# THE ART OF GOLD DIGGING

By
**Tariq "King Flex" Nasheed**

# THE *Art* OF GOLD DIGGING

By
Tariq "King Flex" Nasheed

# TABLE OF CONTENTS

# THE *Art* OF GOLD DIGGING

# Acknowledgments

Taria, Peanut, Joe Rourke, Shawn Calloway, Frank Steelo,

and all the true gold diggers around the world.

# THE *Art* OF GOLD DIGGING

## INTRODUCTION

When people hear the word "gold digger," they automatically conjure up images of a woman who is deceptive, conniving, and manipulative. They also assume that a gold digger is the type of woman who will do any and everything to get over on men and to get money from them *by any means necessary.* This book is going to clear up some of those myths and misconceptions and give you a real understanding about the true art of gold digging.

Ladies, you must first understand there is nothing wrong with wanting the best out of life. Many women have secret desires to wine, dine, shop and travel the world with a man (or men) of means. The reason why many women keep these desires secret is because society often makes it seem morally wrong for a woman to openly express these desires. Since the beginning of time, society has looked down on the woman who wanted it all. More than that, society has done its part in suppressing a woman's desires. This book is going to help you make these desires come true without hiding behind moral smokescreens. This book is going to help you become a guilt-free gold digger.

By and large, women are more attracted to men with money than to men without money. History has shown this to be true. It's something we continue to see everyday-not just in the media-but in our cities and in our neighborhoods. It's a harsh reality that you just have to accept. And you shouldn't have to make any apologies for having that kind of attraction.

This book is not going to teach you how to scam or deceive men out there. I'm going to show you that you don't have to be a cutthroat, scandalous woman, with a scandalous mentality, in order to be a genuine gold digger. Most of the true gold diggers I know are genuinely the nicest, sweetest, most charismatic women you would ever want to meet. They are nothing like the ones you'd see on TV or in the movies. Real gold diggers, unlike their fictional counterparts, have nothing to prove to their peers. They are simply on a different playing field.

I'm going to teach you some of the techniques these true gold diggers use to get men to lavish them with endless riches. **Some of the things that I will teach you in this book will be:**

*The mind state of a gold digger

*Where rich men hang out

*How to attract rich men

*What type of clothes a gold digger should wear

*How to carry yourself around rich men

*What men to avoid

And much, much more.

Now ladies, you might be asking yourself, "How can I learn the art of gold digging *from a man*?" That brings us to **rule number one of the gold digging game:** *Ladies, you cannot learn everything you need to know about the gold digging game from another woman.* Women are naturally competitive with one another. Even if a woman knew everything about the gold digging game, she is more than likely not going to teach you how to potentially outshine her. Most likely, she is not going to share any of her precious information with you. If she is wearing a nice outfit, for example, she's going to be skeptical about sharing information about where she got her outfit with other women. Women like to hold on to their own little secrets about their personal tastes and their personal lives. In the gold digging game, a woman will not purposely create competition for herself. The reason is simple: If she took the time and suffered through the stress and strife of learning the game, she's not going to just give that game away to somebody else and create a level of competition for herself. Much like a great magician not revealing his greatest tricks, she's going to hold on to her secrets. That's part of the reason why there have not been any successful gold digging books out on the market until this one.

Traditionally, there have been two ways for a woman to learn the gold digging game:

1. through luck
2. through trial and error

Now, there have been women who have lucked up and met a rich guy by simply being in the right place at the right time, as was the case of the late Anna Nicole Smith. But this is perhaps a once in a lifetime opportunity. Luck is not something you can plan for. You do not want to depend on luck. You want to depend on strategy. However, the trial and error strategy tends to be mentally and physically tedious. Going about it this way usually takes a woman about five years to learn the ins and outs of the gold digging game. By that time, most aspiring gold diggers have become psychologically and physically worn down from getting into too many hit or miss situations with a number of different men.

This book will help you avoid learning the gold digging game the hard way. You won't have to trudge through five years of misery, searching in vain for that one meal ticket. You won't have to suffer heartbreak after heartbreak looking for the right man. No, by reading this book, I'm going to give you one hundred percent of the gold digging game, because as a man, I am not in competition with you ladies. As a man, I want to see you shine 100% with your game. Moreover, I've spent years writing books, giving lectures, and appearing on television shows teaching men and women different techniques on relationships, dating, and male-female interactions. My methods and expertise have been tried and proven successfully, time and time again.

And ladies, this book will help you upgrade your game and give you access to the secret society of the real, gold digging world.

- TARIQ "KING FLEX" NASHEED

"THERE IS NOTHING WRONG WITH A WOMAN
WELCOMING ALL MEN'S ADVANCES
AS LONG AS THEY ARE IN CASH"

— ZSA ZSA GABOR

# Chapter One

## WHY BE A GOLD DIGGER?

Some critics might ask, "Why write a book about teaching women how to be gold diggers? Why should women learn how to get money from men? Why can't you teach women how to make money on their own?" All of these questions are very valid. There is nothing wrong with a woman putting herself through school, graduating, and working her way up the corporate ladder in order to achieve a significant financial lifestyle. History is rife with notable women who have achieved wealth and power without the need for a man. This is especially true over the past quarter century. However, if you could achieve all that *and* have a wealthy, significant other, then that's icing on the cake. No matter what financial situation you're in, no matter how ambitious or driven you are, there's always a benefit to dating a man of means.

If you are a woman with limited finances, there are obvious benefits from dating a man of means. If you are financially well off, there are still benefits to dating a financially successful man. The both of you, combining your resources, can then become a power couple. In Hollywood, there are many well-known power couples, (such as Brad and Angelina, Will and Jada, Tom and Katie, etc.), who all make a positive impact in the world. They garner a certain level of respect all over the world by being together and utilizing their wealth as couples. Some of the members of these power couples may have previously achieved varying levels of success as individuals. After merging, their combined success often reaches the status of a major corporation or name brand. Without question, there's always a practical reason to date somebody of means.

There are a number of factors that make women want to get into the gold digging game. Once you understand and accept what your true agenda is, you can then tailor your game accordingly.

**The four main reasons why women want to become gold diggers are:**

1. They need the money (which is the obvious reason)
2. They are already accustomed to an upscale lifestyle
3. They want to have a certain status and reputation among family and peers
4. They like the sport of the game

## The Need Of Money

Surprisingly, the least favorable reason for getting into the gold digging game is the need for money. Ladies, you should never get into any endeavor out of necessity. If you start getting with men simply because you need the money or you are desperate for money, you will only think in terms of survival and not strategy. A true gold digger relies solely on strategy. As the saying goes, the worst time to learn how to swim is when you are drowning. When you're drowning, you're going to be kicking, flapping your arms, doing whatever you can do to stay afloat. In that situation, you are truly at the mercy of circumstances. It's best to learn how to swim when you are in control of circumstances.

When you're in survival mode, you make poor choices that you will only regret later. When you're in control, however, your choices are calculated and well thought out. When you're in control, you can swim. So don't wait until you are three days away from getting evicted from your home to decide you want to be a gold digger.

**Being Accustomed To An Upscale Lifestyle**

As I stated before, some women want to get into the gold digging game simply because they have become accustomed to an affluent lifestyle. They may have come from a well-to-do family. Their father or mother may have spoiled them or perhaps, at a very young age, they were catered to by men. And now, they simply want to maintain that lifestyle through the men they date. There is nothing wrong with this. Believe me, it's hard to go from filet mignon to ramen noodles.

**The Desire For Status and Reputation**

Ladies, you should not get into the gold digging game simply because you want to impress your friends or family members. It would be nice to show off and flaunt a rich guy in front of your friends. There's nothing like the thrill of showing up at your high school reunion with a distinguished gentleman in a brand new Bentley.

A little showboating is harmless. But when your primary focus is worrying about what your friends think about you and who you date - this is a sign of major insecurity. To become a true gold digger, you have to rectify all of your insecurities. Otherwise, your achievements as a gold digger - such as they are - will be short-lived.

**Enjoying The Sport Of The Game**

The best reason to get in the game is for the sport of it. Some of the best gold diggers are women who love the thrill of utilizing and executing strategies to keep men catering to their every need. Competitive by nature, these types of gold diggers are just as intrigued by the thrill of the game as they are about the money. Just like the man who is considered a player is more intrigued by the thrill of pursuing and conquering women than he is about the actual sex act, the real gold digger is a woman who respects the game, who respects the art form of gold digging. A woman like this is going to be very, very successful in the game. To succeed in this game, though, you can't just stick your foot in the water to see how cold or deep it is. You have to jump in with both feet. In other words, this game isn't for the timid or the faint of heart.

### Respecting The Game

Ladies, in the gold digging game, it's all about positioning yourselves and having the right knowledge. This book isn't going to give you magic words in order for you to walk up to a rich guy, say some magical phrase, and voila! He's going to give you fifty grand. That's not going to happen in the gold digging game.

To be a true gold digger, it's all about learning the lifestyle. It's all about learning how to respect the game and living the lifestyle and transforming into a true to the game gold digger. But in order to achieve this, you have to play by the rules. The gold digging game is one of the few hustles that has a set of rules that you have to abide by in order to be very successful. This book is going to teach you the real game you need. Now ladies, if your goal is to get a guy to take you to dinner at Applebee's or to buy you a couple of drinks, this book isn't for you. Real gold diggers don't play for food. That's charity work. Real gold diggers play for the big stakes. Real gold diggers go for the gusto. Real gold diggers always have their eyes on the prize.

## Gold Digging and Sex

Ladies, you also need to know that being in the gold digging game is not about giving up sex. You see, real men love challenges. They like the thrill of the chase. They like a woman who is somewhat unattainable. They like a woman who won't put out on the first or second date. So ladies, it's not about sleeping with a large number of men. That's another misconception about the gold digging game. People think that gold diggers are sluts. Of course, it doesn't help that entertainment shows and tabloids gleefully seem to perpetuate that myth. But a true to the game gold digger knows much better than to sleep with a whole bunch of men, especially when traveling in small circles. She knows all too well of this trap. The last thing a gold digger is going to want is having the reputation of being a slut. For a gold digger, being labeled a slut is career ending.

## Staying Focused On Your Gold Digging Goals

The gold digging game is also about common sense. So let's talk about food and drink hustling, which I touched on earlier. When you hustle for a dinner date, that type of insecure hustling is based on ego. The name of the game is about money. As the Godfather himself would say, "It's not personal. It's business." A lot of women try to base their desirability on how many drinks or dinner dates they can get. That's not *real* gold digging. The same energy you put into getting food, you can use that same energy to getting real money. Unfortunately, a lot of women don't see it that way. They want to put in minimal effort and get maximum results. That's gambling in a sense. They want to drop a quarter in the slot machine and hit the jackpot. Just like life, you're going to get out what you put in. If you put in good game, you're going to get good results. True gold diggers have goals. If you have lofty aspirations, you're going to get results based on those aspirations. So while you're trying real hard to get a four hundred dollar meal out of somebody, that four hundred dollars could be in your pocket. And that's with the same amount of effort.

**The Cinderella Syndrome**

Speaking of effort, a lot of women seem to suffer from the Cinderella Syndrome. The story of Cinderella is one of of the most recognized stories around the world, not only because it has been told and retold in countless languages and cultures, but that it's also based on a primal fantasy that a lot of women have. Women who go through hard times in life sometimes think if they dress and pretty themselves up enough, they'll find Prince Charming to come rescue them out of a negative situation. They'll be able to leave their stressful family situation and live happily ever after in the proverbial castle with the man of their dreams.

The Cinderella Syndrome might subconsciously come into play when you date rich guys. If you're dating for food and drinks or you're dating to impress your peers or you're dating just for the thrill of having sex with a rich man, at the end of the day, you're going to go home with nothing. Just like Cinderella, you'll have to "leave the castle," so to speak. Your car is going to turn back into a pumpkin, and you're going to go back to you meager existence. If your quest to success is colored by this fantasy, you will never attain any status worthy of a true gold digger. You have to erase this from your mind, set priorities, and think in terms of long-term income. You have to be very practical if you're going to be a true to the game of gold digger.

Now a lot of people have the impression that it's wrong for a woman to date a guy based on money. As a woman, you have to be practical when it comes to dating. On the other hand, a lot of women will date a guy just because he's cute. After a certain age, you can't have the mentality to date like that because that's how you date when you're in high school. When you're a grown woman, and you have bills and a mortgage and a car note, you can't go to the phone company or mortgage company and try to make a payment with your cute husband or your cute boyfriend. The criterion has to change. You're going to have to bring some tangibles to the game. You have to be more realistic when it comes to dating. You want to get with a man who's going to be the best provider, someone who has the resources to take care of you or upgrade you to the point where you can take care of yourself. Don't get me wrong, cute is always a plus, but that shouldn't be the main criteria. In the long run, cute won't cut it. The bottom line is that you've got to take a truly pragmatic approach to dating and at the same time, step your financial game up.

**The Gold Digger Epiphany**

Many women want to be gold diggers, and they don't even realize it. When these women first become sexually active, some of these thoughts start to develop in their minds. When a woman has sexual relations with the *second* male in her life, to a certain degree that's when the gold digging seeds are planted. You see, when a woman has sex for the first time, usually it's out of love. The woman holds a very sentimental attachment towards the man who takes away her virginity. Now, if that relationship doesn't work out or goes awry, and she happens to have sexual relations with another man, in the back of her mind she's thinking, "Okay, I might have something of value…How can I use this to my advantage?" It's a perception that's in the back of many women's minds. They might suppress it, they might deny it, they might ignore it after awhile, but that thought is always there. When a woman asks herself, "How can I use this to my advantage?" the answer is simply, "Either financially or tactfully." Some women utilize these thoughts more productively than others. The more advantageous a woman is, the more conscious and aware she is with her thoughts and feelings, the more likely she will succeed as a gold digger.

Like I said before, there's nothing wrong with a woman working to get her own money. However, the way a true-to-the-game gold digger looks at it, it's all a matter of perspective. You can work for a boss, a male boss who flirts with you all day, and receive a measly salary of a few hundred bucks a week. By the same token, you can date that same boss (or a man like that boss) and get a few thousand a week

**_Gold Digger_ CHECK LIST #1**

| **TOP 5 DESIGNER CLOTHES FOR GOLD DIGGERS** | 1. BCBG<br>2. GUCCI<br>3. DKNY | 4. BURBERRY<br>5. OSCAR DE LA RENTA |
|---|---|---|

"PEOPLE SAY I'M EXTRAVAGANT
BECAUSE I WANT TO BE
SURROUNDED BY BEAUTY.
BUT TELL ME, WHO WANTS TO BE
SURROUNDED BY GARBAGE?"

— IMELDA MARCOS

# Chapter Two

## GOLD DIGGER BACKLASH

There has been a great deal of backlash against women who use their womanly skills to get money from men. Since the beginning of time, the public has always had a love/hate attitude towards women who are considered gold diggers. Cleopatra was a woman who was admired, but she was ultimately brought down and destroyed because of her gold digging skills. Initially, she had a hard time rising to power, and at one point had to leave Egypt. However, she slowly but surely developed the skills she would need to rule over Egypt once more. Cleopatra used everything she had – exotic sex appeal, intelligence, cunning and wits - and used them in order to get benefits from the two most powerful Romans of her time, Julius Caesar and Marc Antony. As she was a very smart woman, she used a lot of game to get everything she wanted to bring power to her country and to herself. After Caesar was taken out, Cleopatra got together with Mark Antony to solidify her rule over both Egypt and Rome. A lot of Romans resented the way she obtained her power, she didn't bed one Roman legend, but two! And ultimately, those resentful of her brought her down.

**Prehistoric Gold Diggers**

Even before then, in prehistoric times, women had to have game in order to get what they wanted. It was truly a survival of the fittest for these early people. If cavemen wanted something, they would simply use physical force and take what they wanted. Back in those days, prehistoric women couldn't use physical force like that. They had to be more manipulative, especially when dealing with the highly prized, alpha male. The alpha male was the leader of the clan, and for women, he was most likely the best provider, the best lover, and the best at producing healthy children. In order for cavewomen to get what they wanted, they had to use their minds, they had to use their bodies, and last, but not least, they had to use their womanly wits. They had to develop these skills over time. These early gold digging skills are still found in many women. Today, regardless of how internalized these ancient skills may be, some women suppress them. However, there are a number of women today who openly utilize these skills-skills that their ancestors learned before recorded time.

## Renaissance Era Gold Diggers

In prehistoric times women had to learn how to be manipulative. When a woman wanted to get food and shelter, she had to know how to seduce and finesse certain men in order to get those basic needs met. However, the real backlash came into play around the 16th century. Back then, there were women known as courtesans. Courtesans were basically mistresses and kept women who were enjoyed by the rulers and the noblemen of Renaissance Europe at the time. Not exclusive to that part of the world, courtesans served in Asia as well. Here, they were known by other names, such as concubines. For the most part, many powerful men in Europe would get married, but not because they were in love with their wives. Back then, they would get married to preserve a certain bloodline, or they would get married in order to keep royalty in power or for political reasons. These men of means - wealthy, powerful men - would get married to keep certain families in power. But as men, they still had desires. Primal desires. Desires to be with beautiful women. Many of these kings and men of power would live double lives. They would have their wives, but they would also have courtesans on the side.

Some would even escort these courtesans to public events. Many men had lasting relationships with these women. Everybody knew about the courtesans.

After a while, a lot of people, especially women of lower class, started to project their anger and insecurities onto these women. In a given kingdom, women were jealous because they wanted to be in that position. They wanted to be a kept woman. And a lot of the men who weren't financially stable, men who weren't rich-poor men-wanted to get with women like that. Of course they couldn't, because they didn't have the means. So they created a lot of resentment among themselves and other peasants towards these courtesans. These insecure men and women started accusing these courtesans of being evil, manipulative, money and power hungry. They would have public trials accusing these women of being witches, prostitutes, adulterers, etc. They would hold public executions of the courtesans; chop their heads off, burn them at the stake, all kinds of crazy things to these poor women.

In the end, many of the women who escaped these grisly fates had to stay low key with their game to avoid the negative backlash. The women who were considered kept women or mistresses were all looked upon negatively. So in a sense, these women had to go underground and stay below the radar. That negative attitude towards courtesans and gold diggers has lasted to this day.

**Money Is The Root Of All Evil Myth**

People today have a negative attitude towards money or women who get money because they think, "If you do something for money, it's evil." You see, there's a passage in the Bible that is often misquoted. Many misinformed people say, "Money is the root of all evil." But the Bible actually says, "The *love* of money is evil." That's true to a certain degree. If you do certain things purely out of the love or worship of money, or because you lack money, sometimes you start doing evil things. If you do things in a negative way for money, that can be perceived as evil. There's a real big misconception that people who have money are cold and ruthless. But the fact of the matter is, many broke people are cold and ruthless. Go to any impoverished neighborhood anywhere around the world at any given time, and you'll see some of the most cold, ruthless behavior you'll ever want to see in your life. From the slums of America to the shanty towns of a foreign land, you will find the poorest of the poor doing things to their neighbor you wouldn't do to a stray dog. So when people say things like "money is evil," and "people with money are cold and heartless," that's something that broke people say to make themselves feel better.

I can't stress this enough: The backlash against gold diggers is based on good old-fashioned jealousy. Most people have flexible scruples - if they *can* do something that may not be on the up and up but will be profitable for them and they can get away with it, they *will* do that thing. If they can figure out a way to live a better life, they *will* live a better life, no matter how poor they are, no matter how middle class they are. If somebody's broke, and he's hating someone rich or criticizing them for getting out of the 'hood or getting out of poverty, that's insecurity. That's just jealousy talking. When people are in the 'hood or in the streets and they're committing crimes - they're committing crimes for what? For money. They're doing ruthless things in order to get money to come up. Often, other people get hurt in the process. Now if you are a person who plays the game fair and square and you figure out a way to generate a significant stream of income, you shouldn't take heed to any kind of criticism from people who were in the same boat as you when you were on the bottom. Don't fool yourself. If someone can get it, they will get it. If a woman can get money from a man or many men, in most cases, she will. This is nothing to feel bad about.

**Avoiding Haters**

While it's not popular for men to hate other men, it's almost a law of nature for women to hate other women to a degree. Again, women are very competitive with one another. They compete with each other for attention. Most women want to get the best men they can get. For example, if you're a woman working a 9 to 5 job and Brad Pitt or Denzel Washington or George Clooney or any other attractive, multi-millionaire wanted to get with you, most likely you would do it. And if you did, people would label you as a gold digger. But once you're up in a mansion or on an exclusive island, would you really care what people would say about you? That's the point.

Once you get in that position of being a woman of means or a woman who has come up in the game, you really shouldn't care about what haters think. Most real gold diggers don't think about what haters think about them or what jealous women think about them at all. A true to the game gold digger has a thick skin about such things. As a real gold digger, however, you're going to have to learn to get rid of hater-friends.

When you begin to learn the gold digging game and you start to upgrade your lifestyle (looking better, dressing better, traveling, etc.) in many cases you're going to start getting a lot of negative reactions from the people who are closest to you. When you start dating a man of means, and you have friends who are all on the same level as you, then you excel, the people that you were on the same level with before start to feel insecure about themselves. If you start coming up, they're going to say to themselves, "Well, damn, I'm a loser," or, "My friend is doing so much better than me and I'm still here on the bottom!"

Your former friends, instead of looking at their own limited hustle skills, have to find fault in your success to make themselves feel better. Instead of saying, "I need to stop slacking and upgrade my game," they will start saying things like, "Well, she's ruthless," "She's changed," "She's become another person," "She ain't down like she used to be," "She ain't keeping it real no more," or "She's scandalous now." They automatically start projecting their insecurities onto you, their so-called friend, who's trying to better yourself. Women who are true to the game gold diggers have to learn how to play past that and not let that kind of jealous negativity affect them.

Ladies, when you become a true to the game gold digger, you may receive a great deal of backlash. That comes with the territory.

**The people who will give you the most backlash are:**

*Friends              *Women in general

*Family              *Men who think that you're

*Co-workers          out of their league

I know a gold digger, a very good friend of mine, we're going to call her "Lisa." Now, when Lisa was broke, she always had other women around her to share the misery with her. They would always get together and have "pity parties" about how men weren't worth a damn. They would go out to clubs and drink their misery away, party, and get high. Of course they didn't do anything to upgrade themselves and not surprisingly, stayed broke. This was a vicious cycle that continued for some time.

Eventually, Lisa stepped her game up. She started doing a lot better for herself. She started looking fly, and traveled a great deal. Her wardrobe was greatly improved. She upgraded her car. Her friends knew that she was getting money from guys. She didn't care. At first, she wasn't hanging around those broke friends as much, and then, she cut them off completely. Many of these friends that would party, lay up with different men, and get high with Lisa, suddenly started to say how immoral it was for Lisa to get money from men.

In many instances, when women are broke together, they get into all kinds of immoral activity. They get high and sleep with all types of different guys. But all of a sudden, when one person tries to break out of the mold and do something different and better themselves away from the pack, these friends start preaching morality. Sadly, such hypocritical thinking has gotten the best of many would be gold diggers.

**Staying Focused On Your Game**

Lisa realized one important part of the gold digging game:

**It is lonely at the top but it is jam-packed at the bottom**.

Also, you have to remember, it's better to be envied than pitied. See, you can be the typical, struggling martyr. There is nothing more tried and true than the love-struck female who suffers for love, the female who wears her heart on her sleeves, the female who loves hard, the female who's been in and out of many relationships, and last but not least, the female who sacrificed herself for love. That's been played out ad nauseum for as long as men and women have been on this Earth. The bottom line: Gold diggers do not have pity-parties. Misery loves company, but gold diggers will have none of that.

A true to the game gold digger has nothing to complain about because she's getting hers. Don't be apologetic for being about your financial security. Never apologize for wanting to better yourself. Never apologize for not wanting to have a pity-party for yourself. Never apologize for not wanting to sacrifice yourself for the name of love. Tina Turner tried to tell you twenty-five years ago, "What's Love Got To Do With It?" Again, don't be apologetic, because guys out there will not be apologetic for trying to have sex with you once they find out you're an easy target or sucker for love. They will not be apologetic for taking advantage of your fragile state. They will not be apologetic for using you and moving on. As a true to the game gold digger, you must not allow the backlash of haters and naysayers affect your game at all.

*Gold Digger* CHECK LIST #2

| TOP 5 PERFUMES FOR GOLD DIGGERS | 1. CURVE BY LIZ CLAIBORNE<br>2. WHITE DIAMONDS BY ELIZABETH TAYLOR<br>3. LOVELY BY SARAH JESSICA PARKER<br>4. LIGHT BLUE BY DOLCE & GABBANA<br>5. ROMANCE BY RALPH LAUREN |
| --- | --- |

"Love conquers all things
except poverty and a toothache."


— Mae West

# Chapter Three

## TRANSFORMING YOURSELF INTO A GAMESTRESS

Being a gold digger is really a state of mind. It's not simply about me teaching you certain words and certain techniques to remember. That's part of it. But really, the essence of being a gold digger is about having a certain state of mind. It's about having a certain lifestyle that you adhere to. You see, to be a true gold digger, you have to rebuild yourself from scratch. You also have to be a master at relaying ***non-verbal*** language. When you live the lifestyle, you're going to shine in your non-verbal language. That way, you won't come across as being phony. It will all be a natural extension of you. If I just teach you the words and you don't really learn the lifestyle, you're going to second guess some of the things you say. Your words are not going to have the confidence they need to be convincing to your targets out there. So you really have to learn the lifestyle.

**Rebuilding Yourself**

The way to learn the lifestyle is to rebuild yourself, to transform yourself from scratch. You've got to get rid of the old, *square* you, and build yourself up into a brand new, gold digging gamestress. In a way, it's like going into the Army. When you join the Army, they have to build you into a soldier. They have to transform you into a new and better. They have to take you out of your old environment and immerse you in a new environment. They change everything about you in the military. They get you away from your family. They get you away from your old friends. They get you away from your old lifestyle. Instead, they surround you with their peers. They change the way you dress. They change the way you style your hair. They change the way you walk and talk. They change the way you stand. They change the way you use your body language. They change everything about you. And the reason they have to get you out of your old element completely is because they have to start from scratch and build you into a soldier. When it's time to go out there in the field, you're going to be prepared. This always works much better than taking you from your known environment or the environment that you're already familiar with and then preparing you at the last minute. Although it can be a unique learning experience, there's nothing like being taken out of the oven and being thrown into the fire.

But this isn't the ideal way to learn the game. Being immersed in a culture and lifestyle from the get go is ideal. As the hustlers say, "If you stay ready, you don't have to get ready." This is very important to know in order to be a gold digger.

**Upgrading Your Confidence**

Now, the first thing to know about being a gamestress is that you have to have the confidence to try new things. Number one, you've got to have a positive outlook on life. In general, people want to be around other people who are happy. They want to be around people who are perceived as winners. For you to be a successful gamestress, you have to exude confidence. Now, to get confidence-which is the foundation of being a good gold digger-there are few ways to get confidence. Confidence is about trusting yourself. Confidence is about being sure about your decisions. It is about being sure about your own self-image. Unfortunately, a lot of people don't have a positive self-image. They have failed so much in life that they don't understand the concept of achieving any goals. They just accept failure. For them, failure almost becomes comfortable. If you want to have confidence, you too have got to become uncomfortable with failing.

Building confidence is very simple when you understand the basic meaning of confidence. **Confidence is about trusting yourself.** Self trust. You see, you don't question why you have confidence in other people. This is because you trust them. At work, you trust your boss is going to pay you a paycheck. That's one of the reasons why you work for your boss. You trust your pastor at church because you know that he's going to be consistent and follow through. You trust and have confidence in certain people because you know that they're going to be consistent in what they say and what they do. You should have that same trust in yourself if you want to be a real, true gamestress.

Another major way to build confidence is setting goals. You can start off by setting small goals, achieving those goals, knocking those goals out, and moving onto more challenging goals. The more you accomplish, the more confidence is built up. It's like building a skyscraper, with each small goal as a brick. The more bricks you build with, the higher your confidence and self esteem will be. You will trust in yourself that you can achieve anything you want to achieve. Again, it could be a very small goal that you set for yourself initially. When you achieve that goal, you're going to feel real good about yourself. This is a simple but highly effective way to build confidence. For example, you can say to yourself, "From now on, I'm going to exercise twenty minutes every day." And if you do that every day, you're going to feel better and more confident about yourself. You can also say, "I want to take up a cooking class," "I want to learn French," "I want to build a website," "I want to start a business," "I want to record an album," or "I want to paint my house." It could be something as small as taking one day to pay your bills. If you set a goal to pay all your bills in one day, and you go out and do it, at the end of the day, you're going to feel better about yourself. You're going to say to yourself, "Okay, I did that. I got off my butt and I did something that I said I was going to do." And that gives you the confidence to want to try to do other things.

You see, the idea is for you to get up off the couch and go out to do things. Sometimes, the hardest thing is finding the motivation to achieve certain goals. Even with the relatively simple goal of going to the gym, the hardest part is actually leaving your house. Once you leave your house and you get to the gym, you're good. You're going to go in there and do what you have to do. That applies to any other goal that you're trying to achieve. As I've mentioned before, the easiest way to build confidence is to set a lot of goals and achieve those goals. You start off small and then you build up to bigger, more challenging goals. As a gamestress, your objective is to transfer and apply that confidence to the gold digging field.

To be a real gamestress, there's a period in time where you have to go through what I call a "the hell with it" moment. Every woman-if she wants to be successful at anything, especially in the gold digging game-is going to have to go through a "the hell with it" moment. When you're constantly trying to please everybody and you're trying to seek approval, not only does this show a lack of confidence, this is a pathway to failure. You're simply not going to please everybody. And if you notice, the more people you try to please when you try to cater to every single person and not offend everybody, the more criticism you end up receiving. At a certain point in your life, you're going to have a "the hell with it" moment, where you say, "You know what? I try hard to please everybody and I'm still getting criticism. Let me just make my own decisions and do what works for me. If I offend some people, so be it." Once you have that epiphany, you're on your way to becoming a grade A gamestress, and a true to the game gold digger. Because no matter what you do, some people are just going to just get offended. That's just part of life.

Now there is nothing wrong with helping and assisting others in need. But don't go out of your way to be a people pleaser, especially when the people you are trying to please aren't doing anything for you or looking out for your best interest.

**Think About Success**

Another way to become a gamestress is to think about success all the time, think about being a winner all the time. By all the time, I really mean today. Too many people say to themselves, "I'll be happy later." They have a delayed happiness thing going on in their minds. You have to be comfortable and pleased and satisfied with yourself today, first and foremost in order for you to be confident and in order for you to be happy. That vibe is going to resonate from you when you  meet new people. Especially rich people. Many of them have a sixth sense in determining the level of happiness in those around them. I've heard women say, "When I get married I'll be happy then," "If I date a football player, I'll be happy then," "If I get two hundred dollars, I'll be happy then." You have to live that joyous lifestyle right now. You have to feel like you deserve the best. That will attract the vibe of success.

Ladies, if you don't have that winning mentality, you're not going to appreciate what you get, simply because you don't appreciate what you have. Because, like I said before, so many women are used to losing and failing, when they come into a winning situation,they can't appreciate it because it feels uncomfortable. As a gamestress, you have to get over the losing streak mentality when it comes too dating wealthy men.

### Don't Be A Fence Sitter

Now ladies, if you want to be a gold digger and a gamestress, you cannot be what we call a "fence sitter." You can't be a square *and* in the game. You cannot have one foot in the game, and one foot in the square world. You're going to have to be in one or the other. There are plenty of women out there who are fence sitters. Women who live out their entire lives in safe situations, only dreaming of life "on the other side." Some of them try to explore the other side in secret. But this tends to be half-assed.

If you want to have a square relationship -a so-called boyfriend - and then sneak around and have a sugar daddy on the side, that's half-assed hustling. When you're in a situation like that, the square guy that you're dating-the unknowing guy-isn't going to approve of you being in another relationship with a sugar daddy. Ninety eight percent of the guys out there aren't going to go for that. There are a lot of women in those situations, and a lot of these women are more intrigued by the thrill of being *deceptive* instead of the thrill of getting money.

When you're in a situation where you're fence-sitting-you have a square relationship and you're trying to have a "sugar daddy on the side," you're not going to be one hundred percent thorough with your game. Most of your focus is going to be covering your tracks and not being found out by your square significant other. You get in what you put out of a situation. If you put half-assed energy into the game, you're going to get half-assed results.

In order to be a thorough gamestress and get maximum results, you have to live this lifestyle one hundred percent. For now, you have to drop the square relationship entirely. You can always parlay the knowledge of being in the lifestyle later on down the line when you want to square up and get married or have a one on one, monogamous relationship with a guy who you're in love with. But if you're going to be in the game right now, and get real results, you have to be in it to win it.

**Change Your Environment**

To be a good gamestress and a good gold digger, you have to change your environment. You have to put yourself in a productive, positive environment. You see, in nature every living creature will physically and psychologically adapt to its own environment or to the environment that it comes to live in if it's going to survive. That's why a chameleon turns into the color of the environment it is in. Other animals will adapt to the environment they're in. The same condition exists with human beings. If you broke, living in an impoverished environment, that's what you're going to keep attracting. If you are in an abusive environment, abusive things are going to keep happening to you. However, if you are placing yourself in an environment of wealth, eventually some of that wealth will come to you. If you are living in a positive, upscale environment, or you place yourself in that environment - even if you don't have a lot of money -eventually your mind will adapt and get used to being in that environment. That positive energy of wealth will start coming to you.

As they say, there's only one law in the universe, and that's the law of attraction. Everything else falls under various sub-categories.

You have to stay in a progressive, positive environment if you want that wealth energy to fall into your lap. You have to stay away from petty, negative environments. You have to stay away from gossipy environments. You have to stay away from envious environments. You wouldn't want any of that energy to rub off on you. Go to upscale places, hang out around upscale people in upscale places. If you can place yourself there physically, you will get there mentally,and ultimately financially.

**No Narcotics**

To be a successful gold digger, you also have to be drug-free. Right now, being a marijuana smoker is the "in thing". Weed-head women are not attractive. Men - especially wealthy men - can tell if a woman is a weed-head. Weed makes you look cheap. Of course, we all know weed is a very common drug. But does that make it acceptable to use? Now, meth and crack and other hard drugs are completely out of the question, that goes without saying. But many women think that weed isn't a drug. They think that because it grows as a plant, it's natural. Well, if we took that reasoning and applied it to other areas, snake venom is natural. Arsenic is natural. So is curare. Just because something is natural doesn't mean it's good for you. Inhaling smoke in the body is the most unnatural thing that you can do. Saying that weed is natural is just an excuse - a cop-out. Just because something is natural doesn't mean that you have to put it in your body.

Most upscale men are not going to invest in a woman who's a weed-head. Another thing-a lot of weed-head women don't think that they look like weed-heads. They have the delusion that their looks aren't affected by weed. Truth be told, weed affects your looks. Weed affects your actions. The only men with money who really want to be with or invest in weed-heads are weed dealers or drug dealers. They don't really want to have a serious relationship with a weed-head themselves. The bottom line for an aspiring gold digger: Any kind of drug use is completely out of the question. That's not indicative of good gold digger behavior.

A gold digger's greatest tool is her mind. You don't want to do anything to alter your greatest tool. You don't want to do anything that's going to alter your mind or compromise your thinking because that's the first thing men will try to test you with. When men offer drugs, they want to see how loose you are. They want to see how easy you are. And in their eyes, if you accept any kind of drugs, that means you're weak.

That means you're an easy target. And they've got you. Once they get the drug or drugs in you or once they see you're susceptible to any kind of drug use - Bam! Game over. They are now in control of the situation. A gold digger and a gamestress are always in control of the situation.

**Upgrading Your Fitness Game**

Now ladies, here's a harsh reality: Most rich men generally don't date out of shape women. A man wants his woman's beauty to match his wealth. If he's *financially* disciplined, he wants a woman who's at the very least *physically* disciplined. Wealthy men think like winners. And winners love trophies that show off the fact that they are winners. We always hear the cliché about the trophy wife or the trophy girlfriend. Rich men want women that represents their wealth. That's going to show people how fly he is. That woman is his representative, in a sense. So you have to have your look together.

Now, there are some women who are thick or may be slightly overweight who can get money. In situations like that, her game has to be so tight that it overcompensates her lack of tip top physical fitness. In most cases, though, a man of means wants a woman who is the most attractive. You have to go out there and have the discipline and the consistency to hit the gym on a regular basis. If you go to upscale places around the country, like the Hamptons, you will find women jogging early in the morning. If you go to Beverly Hills at six or seven in the morning, you'll see women running and jogging. If you go to Malibu, you'll see women jogging down the beach. Women in these rich neighborhoods know that they have to stay in shape in order to stay in these neighborhoods. So, if you're serious about the game, you have to hit that gym. You have to be very cognizant of your physical attributes and keep them maintained all the time. Many of these women are fully aware that if they don't stay in shape,their wealthy significant other will eventually replace them with the next female who has it together.

*Gold Digger* CHECK LIST #3

**TOP 5 CARS FOR GOLD DIGGERS**

1. LEXUS SC 430
2. RANGE ROVER
3. MERCEDES SLK
4. ROLLS ROYCE PHANTOM COUPE
5. CORVETTE

"NATURE SAYS TO A WOMAN:
'BE BEAUTIFUL IF YOU CAN,
WISE IF YOU WANT TO,
BUT BE RESPECTED, THAT IS ESSENTIAL."

— BEAUMARCHAIS

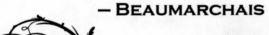

# *Chapter Four*

## UNDERSTANDING YOUR TARGETS

Now, ladies, when it comes to the gold digging game, you have to know the mindset of the men you're dealing with out there. You have to know how your targets think, how they maneuver, how they interact with each other, what your targets do for a living, and how they got their money. It's also very important to understand the different types of wealthy targets that are out here in the gold digging game.

I'm going to break the wealthy targets down into six categories. There may be some variation, but these six are the standards from which we can draw upon. We'll call them the **Six "Ls."** They are:

1. The Ladies' Man;

2. The Lieutenant;

3. The Lackey;

4. The Love-struck Target;

5. The Laid-back Target; and

6. The Lowlife Target.

Let's break these categories down, one by one.

### The Ladies Man

This wealthy target is the James Bond/Playboy type. He uses his affluence to his full advantage. He's the rich, old-school playboy, like Tony Stark from the movie Iron Man. He loves the jet-set lifestyle. He loves being single and definitely loves to play the field. A true lover of women, he tends to juggle a number of them. An adventurous guy like this looks for his opposite in a woman, in order to give him balance. Because of this, you have to be somewhat stable. You don't have to necessarily be the polar opposite of the Ladies' Man, but he is looking for a balance when it comes to a woman.

Now, when the Ladies' Man deals with women, it's all about the challenge. He likes the thrill of the chase. He likes the competitiveness of winning a woman over. The rich Ladies Man has had his share of disposable floozies. In order for you to counteract this, you have to play the square, goody-two-shoes role. You don't want to be another one of the Ladies' Man's conquests. You really have to be on top of your game with him because he knows how women think. You also never want to come across as being impressed by his wealth or his smooth demeanor. Often either a millionaire or a billionaire, the Ladies' Man sole interest is to impress women. Not surprising, his house is completely decked out. No matter what, **try not to act overly impressed with the Ladies' Man's surroundings or his antics.** Again, you've got to really be on top of your game when you deal with the Ladies' Man.

## The Lieutenant

The Lieutenant is a very strict, by the book, suit and tie type of guy. He is probably a lawyer, a psychologist, a doctor, or an executive working in corporate America. He might even be a politician. Everything is very clean-cut and straight and narrow with this guy. You have to be very tactful when dealing with the Lieutenant. You want to kind of be a balance for him, but you don't want to go too liberal or too wild. On the other hand, you want to bring out his wild side, because the Lieutenant can be somewhat of a tight ass. You have to be that fun balance for him.

However, as I mentioned before, you can't go over the top with him or you'll turn this guy off. With the Lieutenant, if he wants to spend serious time with a woman, he'll give money to her if she can somewhat fit into his social circle. Ironically, many Lieutenants have off the wall fetishes. Since they live by such a strict, by the book lifestyle, they repress their crazy fantasies. As many of us know, the more you repress and push something down, the more it's going to burst and push its way out that much harder. That's why we have a lot of conservative politicians such as governors and senators getting caught up in sex scandals.

In recent years we have seen some of the most openly conservative politicians and public figures get exposed for things like ordering prostitutes, soliciting gay sex in restrooms,etc. On one hand, they represent the face of conformity, and on the other, they hide their twisted desires. You have to serve as a delicate balance for the Lieutenant. You might actually have to walk on eggshells with this guy. But once you find a good  Lieutenant that you have a compatible vibe with,the pay off is worth it.

## The Lackey

A Lackey is one of those trust fund guys, a guy who got his money through his family fortune. Real laid back, he's basically living off mom and dad. He's the spoiled rich kid who likes to get drunk and get high all day. He likes to play video games all the time. A guy like this is most likely not self-made. He looks for a surrogate mother when it comes to dating. You have to mother the rich Lackey guy, literally and figuratively. You don't want to indulge in any of his goofy little activities, at least to a certain degree. You can engage in some, but you don't want to fall into the trap of becoming another lackey like him. If you do,eventually, he's going to get bored with you and find another lackey female to spend time with.

As with the Lieutenant, you have to serve as a balance for the Lackey. On one hand, you have to get him off the couch. You have to motivate this guy. On the other hand, you don't want to appear to scold him or show him any negative attributes that may remind him of his mother. With the Lackey, you do have to mother him, but understand he's very rebellious towards his parents. You don't want to push this guy to the point of him rebelling against you. You don't want him to rebel against you at all. It's key for you to be a delicate balance, or the maternal-lover-friend for the Lackey.

Also, when I mentioned that you engage in some of his activities, I don't mean engage in drug use that Lackeys engage in. I also don't mean you ought to get drunk with them all the time. You're not going to get any money out of this guy this way. If you show him that you're just a lackey like him, he's going to lump you with the rest of the slackers who tries to leech off him. The objective is to get this guy to see you as somebody worthy of giving money to.

**The Love Struck Target**

Now, the Love-struck Target can be any type of personality, he can come from any kind of financial background, but these guys are considered hopeless romantics. These guys really believe in the old school idea of love. They probably had parents who have been together for a number of decades. They want that family life, that white picket fence life.

Unfortunately, being rich, they attract a lot of seedy, needy women. Blinded by their preconceived notions of romance, they're looking for that Miss-goody-two-shoes type of woman to wife up. Not surprisingly, these guys are very, very good targets-that is, if you can get them before the other girls do. They tend to get scooped up very quickly. Countless women look for these Love-struck Targets. Women feast on guys like this. It's like throwing meat in a pool of piranha. When these women see there's a rich guy looking for love, they eat that up. These are the kind of guys who want to go on very romantic dates. Many of them might be a little on the nerdy side. Not the most social of butterflies, they spend a good deal of time working on their financial skills and trade skills-whatever brings them money. When it comes to social skills, these guys try to go old school and ultra romantic. They don't know how to balance that out. They don't know the definition of "over the top." You can jump on these guys very easily.

**The Laid Back Target**

The Laid-back Target, to a certain degree is a combination of the Ladies' Man and the Lieutenant. These guys are not called "laid back" because they're getting high on weed or wasted on alcohol. These guys are called "laid back" because they have a cool, mellow demeanor. They're unassuming. They dress casually. They're likely to be very quiet and hush-hush about how they got their money. They don't brag, they don't front, and they don't floss. They're not flashy-not in any sense of the word. They simply sit back and observe everything. They're smart, intellectual guys, but they're not too square, not at all like the Love-

THE ART OF GOLD DIGGING

struck Target. As a matter-of-fact, they're not nerdy at all. They're just peeping you out, seeing what's going on in the scene. They like to kick back and peep their surroundings.

Laid-back Targets are sociable, to a certain degree. They're not as slick as the Ladies' Man, but do have a certain swagger. That's why you have to have your guard up a little when you first deal with them. You have to play psychological and mental chess with these guys, because they're looking at you thinking of how they're going to make their move. They're also trying to figure out what your moves are. You need to be doing the same thing. You need to keep yourself a mystery with these guys. The less they know about you-at least initially - the better. At the same time, you've got to bring them out of their laid-back shell. You've got to bring them out of their laid-back element. Don't let them bring you out of your element, because they're going to try to make you move across the chessboard. The objective for you is to make them move across the chessboard. You want to create a sense of intrigue about yourself that will draw the Laid Back Target into you.

**The Low Life Target**

The Low-life is a rich guy who kind of lucked up on his money.

He might be a guy who's a drug dealer. He might be a guy who made a lot of money selling cocaine, or made a lot of money selling marijuana. He might be a guy who's made his fortune as a money embezzler or jewel thief (I have personally known a few guys back in the day who were jewel thieves and they actually made a lot of money). He might be a guy who is an art thief, stealing expensive paintings. There are plenty of guys out there like that. These type of guys are often portrayed in gangster movies (like Goodfellas, Scarface, etc.). The bottom line: The Low-life Target is a guy who has made a lot of money in an illicit way. He may have blackmailed somebody or might be in the process of blackmailing somebody. He might have gotten a sex tape or pictures from a celebrity and sold them to the highest bidder.

There are a lot of guys like this in Hollywood and New York—especially in Hollywood. There are a lot of guys like this who've made a lot of money dealing in porn. You've got to watch out for guys like this, because, even though they have a lot of money, they still have low-life characteristics. They can get you caught up in a negative situation at any moment, caught up in their world. The Low-life Target always has to watch his back. If you're in their world, something might happen to you by proxy, by association. So you want to avoid the Low Life Target because you never want to be in a situation where you have to watch your back.

### Dealing With The Six L's

You have to really change your game up when you're dealing with the six "Ls." The biggest mistake women make when they're dealing with the six "Ls" is that they try to deal with all these guys the same way. You can't deal like that. That's like playing the Lottery when it comes to dating. I know a young lady named Linda, who was very aggressive with most of her targets. With some targets, you do have to be aggressive. For example, you have to be very aggressive with the Lackey. With the Love-struck Target, you have to be aggressive with him as well because he looks for a woman who's a domineering figure-a mother figure.

Linda was not only aggressive with the Lackey and Love-struck Target, but was very aggressive with the Lieutenant and the Ladies' Man. That approach doesn't work on all targets. The Ladies' Man doesn't want an aggressive woman like that. The Lieutenant definitely doesn't want an aggressive woman like that because they're going to butt heads. Linda would have hit-or-miss relationships with the different targets she would date and deal with. When you have a hit-or-miss vibe with your targets, that becomes frustrating. You want to keep your energy. You don't want to waste your energy on situations that are not working, because number one, that's a blow to your confidence. Number two, it tires you out, creating a sense of bitterness. To be a true gold digger, you have to flow and you have to be tactful. You have to be a chameleon with your game. You have to know when to change your game up and deal with your targets accordingly. That is very, very important. Every target is a custom job. You have to approach each and every one with both eyes open.

**Understanding Your Agenda**

Now ladies, when you are getting into the gold digging world, there are basically three main agendas:

1. money
2. thrill and adventure
3. marriage

When you deal with your different targets, you have to be very clear in your mind what your agenda is. If you're not clear with what your agenda is, you're not going to be clear on whom to target and with whom to get what from what. If your primary agenda is money, it's best for you to deal with the Lieutenant. It's going to be really difficult to get the Ladies' Man to commit, so you need to get in quick and get out quick. These guys are good targets if you are seeking adventure. With the money thing, you sometimes have to juggle different targets.

If you're going to juggle targets, it's best to juggle the Lieutenant and the Lackey. That would be a safe combination to handle. An unsafe target to handle would be the Low-life. Many women are turned on to the dangerous , unpredictable lifestyle of the rich Low-life. But as a gold digger, you should never put yourself in a situation where your well-being will be at stake.

In the next chapter, I'm going to address some of the rich targets who you need to stay away from. If you are more intrigued by thrill and adventure, you should also target men European or other foreign accents. European, Latin American, and Australian guys for example, are very adventurous. They love to travel; they love to gamble; they love to bungee jump, hang glide, parasail, scuba dive,etc. They love to do all kinds of crazy, adventurous things. If you really want adventure in a target, steer more towards the foreign ones. If they're here from another country,in many cases that means they have a love for and are used to traveling. They love taking women with them as they go around the world. They like to impress you with their knowledge of the world. They like to get into hot air balloons, they like to go deep-sea fishing in the Caribbean, they like to go mountain climbing in the French Alps, they like to go shark hunting in Australia.

Foreign guys are the best as far as thrill and adventure. Now, if you want marriage, you've got to be very careful. Don't be blinded by your own desires and try to put the wrong man into the marriage category. You don't want to play the numbers game when it comes to marriage. If you're just trying to get money, it's cool to play the numbers game. Again, you can have a number of guys who you're juggling.

However, if you're trying to get married to a guy, you have to understand it is a small world. If your name is floating around all of these rich guys' circles, and you're trying to convince one of them you're marriage material, that's not a good look. You have to choose correctly out the gate if you want to get a guy and hook him up for marriage. You've got to do your research on a target and the social circles that he's in. Once you lock in on a target, it would be difficult for you to go back to that same circle and try to get more guys because your name is already known in that circle.

Again, you really have to do your research. It can't be hit or miss. It's like betting on a horse: it's all gambling, but when you bet, you can study the horses and see who has a good track record; you can study the thoroughbred of the horse; you can study the owner of the horse; you can study some of the races the horse has been in before you make your bet on that horse so you make an educated gamble. And that's what you want to do with a rich guy whom you're trying to marry. You have to make a very educated gamble when you deal with this guy, so you have to choose correctly out the gate.

**Small Things To Look For With Targets**

There are certain things to look for in your targets. One thing you want to look for is men with manicures. Manicures are very important. If you see a man with a manicure that means that he likes to present himself in a certain way. Look at those fingernails. When you see a guy with nice hands that shows that he's not doing manual labor. Now, there's nothing wrong with a man doing manual labor, but you, the gold digger, want to get a guy who is sitting on millions. Most millionaires just don't do manual labor. They have other guys doing the grunt work.

Also, you want to look for a guy who wears nice shoes. This may sound a little clichéd, but most rich guys take pride in the shoes that they wear. That's very big with rich guys. Look at his jewelry. You don't want a guy whose jewelry is too gaudy, look for the real Rolex watch. A lot of guys who try to act rich will go and get a fake Rolex watch, and some women fall for it. One way you can tell, ladies, if a Rolex watch is real: the second hand of a genuine Rolex watch does not tick. In most watches, the second hand will tick. The Rolex hand *floats* - it never ticks. That's a sure fire way to see if a Rolex watch is real. Another thing about jewelry: There are certain rich guys who like to pile on the jewelry, flashy rings and expensive chains. Rap artists come to mind. I will address this group in the next chapter.

Of course, there are targets who purposely try to dress down to hide their wealth. They might drive an average looking car and look like they work on a farm. But you can tell they're loaded. Follow them around town and see where they hang out. They might be driving that bucket to the yacht club. They might spread their wealth in several different banks and investment houses. These targets might be men who lost some of their wealth to an ex-wife and are trying to go incognito. These targets might just be worth a shot. But remember, **the flashiest guy is not always the richest guy**. It's natural for many women to be attracted to flash. But always keep an eye out for the small things. Because the casually dressed guy sitting at the bar could be an undercover millionaire.

*Gold Digger* CHECK LIST #4

| TOP 5 MAKE-UP/ COSMETIC PRODUCTS FOR GOLD DIGGERS | 1. MAC<br>2. L'OREAL<br>3. ESTÉE LAUDER<br>4. LANCÔME<br>5. CLINIQUE |
|---|---|

## "FOR EVERY MAN THERE EXISTS A BAIT WHICH HE CANNOT RESIST SWALLOWING."

## — FRIEDRICH NIETZSCHE

# Chapter Five

## WHO NOT TO TARGET

Ladies, we all know there are plenty of guys out there with great character. This chapter isn't meant to lessen or disregard a person's character or occupation. But in the gold digging game, you have to be very strategic about whom you target and whom you stay away from if you're trying to get money. Now most rich guys regardless of title or occupation are fair game. But there are some men with money and some men in general you may want to avoid (or men you shouldn't place too much focus on). Those men are:

**Athletes**

Most women who chase after athletes are often miscategorized as gold diggers. Interestingly enough, most women who chase after athletes are not gold diggers, because often times getting money is not on their agenda. They might lie and say that they get money from certain athletes in order to look good to their peers. These women who chase after athletes in all actuality do not get money. These women are considered *groupies*. Now, there's a big difference between being a gold digger and a groupie. You never want to be considered a groupie. A gold digger is trying to get the money, plain and simple. The groupie is trying to get the reputation and the status. The best way you can tell the difference between a gold digger and a groupie is through observation. If you go to a club and see a bunch of women talking to two or three athletes, those women are groupies. If you see a woman sitting at the bar talking to the *owner of the team,* she's a gold digger. You always want to be a gold digger with your game. You don't want to sweat athletes and getting labeled as something you're not. Athletes can get sex easily, and these groupies will do anything they want them to do. Athletes have no want or need to give groupies money.

Most of the women who hang around athletes do it because they think it makes them look important. These women are easily impressed. Oftentimes, dealing with athletes is a waste of time for a true to the game gold digger. Moreover, many athletes come from backgrounds where it was difficult for them to get money. When they go pro and finally come into money, they hold on to it. Add to this the fact that they have their families, their friends, and associates with their hands out. Literally everyone is in their pockets. This leaves the athletes on the defensive. You do not want to add fuel to that fire and get into the difficult task of trying to get money from them. You want to avoid that altogether.

On the other hand, if you want to get bragging rights in the 'hood, knock yourself out. Athletes usually have serious relationships with women who already comes from a wealthy background,female celebrities,and women they were with before they had money. Now if a rich athlete is seriously checking for you,by all means proceed to get your foot in the door financially. But a true gold digger will not focus so much on athletes.

**Recently Divorced Men**

Other guys whom a gold digger should not target are recently divorced guys. Many of these guys are going through a great deal of financial difficulties. They might be paying alimony. They might be paying for a house they no longer own and for another they're presently living in. They might be paying for a second or third mortgage because of their present state of affairs. They might also be paying child support. They're definitely going to be paying a lawyer. Again, these guys may be seriously having financial difficulties. You're not going to get any kind of long-term money from a recently divorced guy, unless everything was cut off clean and clear. That is, he had a pre-nup, his money is still straight, and he's on top of his game. That's the only exception.

Most guys who are divorced, if they're going through difficulties, will usually let you know what's going on if you just talk to them. If you meet a divorced guy, screen him thoroughly within the first hour or even within a few minutes of talking to him, and find out where he is financially. You can do that in a smooth, subtle way without coming across as a gold digger. Regardless of the outcome, you want to be seen as having class, and not tacky. You definitely do not want to remind him of the ex he's paying.

**Flashy Men**

Other guys to avoid are guys who are too flashy. Most of these guys, who dress in gaudy outfits and trying to display money, are not really rich. They put on a front to look rich but most genuinely rich guys are actually kind of low-key. Wealthy men dress clean and they're well groomed, but they generally dress down. They're not flashy; they don't wear loud colors; and they don't display over the top jewelry. For the most part, they're quite subdued.

## School Teachers

If you are on the hunt for men with money, you want to avoid men who are schoolteachers. If you meet a guy who's a schoolteacher, in many cases he's broke. It's that simple. Most schoolteachers, unfortunately, don't make a lot of money. Unless they're a tenured professor at a university, teachers are not paid well. Great guys, but they are not affluent by any means. They might not always be broke, but they don't have the serious kind of money a gold digger is after.

## Rappers

Ladies, you want to seriously avoid rappers. Now, when you deal with entertainers, the types of entertainers you want to go for are actors -by this, I mean *working* actors, producers, singers (R & B singers or even pop singers), and even screenwriters (those with verifiable credits). Rappers offer a tricky situation. Surprisingly, most rappers don't have the kind of money you'd think they have. Unless they've been in the game for a while and made sound investments, these rappers simply don't have a lot of money. It's like dating an athlete without the money. Rappers are infamous for renting houses, leasing cars, and flossing a bunch of assets they don't own. Rappers also tend to surround themselves with scavenger type people who give no second thought to spending their money. The girls who date rappers tend to be groupies. They date them for the bragging rights. They date them so they can get a role in a video and props in the hood. On the contrary, a gold digger wouldn't be caught dead on anybody's video set. A true to the game gold digger will try her best to avoid rappers.

**Other Characteristics To Look Out For**

There are a few other types of guys to stay away from that I will touch on briefly. With these guys we focus less on occupation and more on personal characteristics. For example, guys you need to avoid are alcoholics. They may be wealthy but they can be loose cannons. Under the influence, they may become belligerent. Alcoholics have no control over their lives when they drink. Other guys you want to stay away from are bohemians. These are the herbal tea sipping, dreadlock sporting, incense burning, poetry reading guys. These guys are usually broke.

You also want to avoid verbally abusive guys. When targets are verbally abusive, and they start making threats, or they say cruel things to you, you've got to go. You don't deal with men like that, men who obviously have psychological or anger issues. When you're involved with a verbally abusive man, it may only be a matter of time before he becomes physically abusive. Men like that tend not to change, at least not for the better. Let the square girls deal with that. Other guys you want to stay away from are sales or marketing guys who focus their skills on telemarketing or some other phone-based business. These guys will not have money. Period.

Ladies, this is a very tricky group to avoid: **Gay guys**. Now, I don't say that to diss gay guys or to question their character. But when you're out in social settings, you might meet a few gay guys who you have no idea are gay. They'll strike up a conversation with you, and a decent one at that. Gay guys have no problem at all chatting with a very attractive woman, because they don't have a fear of rejection. They're not out to get anything from you. They can strike up a conversation with an attractive woman at the drop of a hat-especially with an attractive, model type. Gay guys love models and other beautiful, sophisticated women. In some cases, gay guys want to talk to these women to soak up the mannerisms. Many may not be your stereotypical, over the top, flaming gay guys. But you don't want to waste your time talking to a guy you're not going to get anything from, when you could be working the room on some potential straight targets. That's why I say don't talk to gay guys or don't be misled by talking to an undercover gay guy. If you're talking and flirting with a guy, and he's gay, you're not going to get anything out of the deal.

That being said, there is nothing wrong with having gay friends. As a matter of fact, if you befriend a gay guy, he might take you into some of his social circles. If he's your buddy-and everybody knows that you guys are buddies and he's introducing you to people-he will willingly provide you with a good way to get your foot in the door with the elite. Gay guys in Hollywood, Miami and New York are really hooked into wealthy circles. They are truly connected with the rich and powerful. Moreover, many gay dudes are well groomed and very well dressed. Many of them keep their nails impeccably done, their hair flawlessly cut , and their clothes tailored to perfection. Not only do they look wealthy, many of them are wealthy. But even the ones who are not wealthy look like money because they really, really take pride in taking care of themselves.

### Clues To Tell If Your Target Might Be Gay

Now, if you're talking to a guy and you're getting some clues and some gay vibes but you're not sure, you can always ask him about what he does for a living. That's a simple way to screen him. There are gay guys who are employed in all kinds of occupations. There are gay doctors, lawyers, judges, cops, and athletes. In short, there's gay everything. But I'm going to give you *five occupations to look out for that will let you know that most likely the guy is gay.*

### Number One: A Hairdresser

Now, there are straight male hairdressers - very few - but they're out there. If he says he's a barber, there's a big difference. Barbers tend to be straight, catering to a straight male clientele. If he says he's a hairdresser, however, he is most likely gay. Now I do know some straight male hairdressers who use their occupation as a way to sleep with a number of their female clients. But these guys are far and between.

### Number Two: A Makeup Artist

Personally, I've never met a straight male makeup artist. There may be exceptions to the rule, but if you meet a gentleman and he tells you that he's a make up artist, congratulations; you have a new gay friend.

### Number Three: An interior Decorator

A lot of gay guys are decorators. This is a very popular occupation in the gay community. Gay guys are no joke when it comes to decorating.

### Number Four: A Fashion Stylist

There are countless gay guys working in the fashion industry. Fashion stylists tend to be highly specialized in their field, and are almost always gay.

### Number Five: Pet Groomer

If you meet a guy and he's a pet groomer or he owns a pet grooming business, seven times out of ten he's gay. Sure there are some straight pet groomers out there, but from my observations, professional pet groomers are gay.

Again, this isn't saying anything negative about gay guys. You just don't want to flirt with a guy who's more interested in what type of shoes and purse you're wearing. The only gay exception - and there is an exception - for dealing with and getting money from a gay guy, is a gay guy who's still in the closet or unsure about his sexuality. He wants what is called a "beard." A gay man gets a female front to make him appear to be straight. He gets a girlfriend or a wife and parades her around to give family and friends the impression that he's heterosexual. In a situation like this, you can get some serious money. You can be a professional, well-paid beard for a gay guy. Depending on the specific situation, you can let him know that you're in on the scheme or not. It can be a covert operation. It doesn't have to be overt. It can be a general understanding that you guys have. You'll play the girlfriend or wife role with this guy, but he has to compensate you for your time. This is a given. Again, this is the only exception regarding dealing with a gay guy. Otherwise, you are wasting your time.

**Other Targets To Avoid**

Other targets who you need to avoid are **braggarts**-guys who brag about how much money they have. Guys like this are most likely not rich. There's an old saying that talkers never do, and doers never talk.

Guys who have a lot of money don't have to brag about it, because you can see the money. You can see it in their mannerisms. You can see it in their words and actions. Most important, you could see it in their lifestyle. If a braggart says that he's a doctor and he's driving a beat up Honda Civic, most likely he is fronting. If you meet a guy and he says he's a Hollywood producer, but he looks scraggly, wears clothes that fell off a truck, and lives in a bad part of town, those are clear indicators that he's a braggart. You have to cross-reference their words, their non-verbal language, and their lifestyle, and you'll soon find out if he's the real deal or not. Again, there are exceptions to the rule-like the new doctor who drives an older Honda to pay off his student loans - but that is the exception.

**Church Guys**

You also want to avoid church guys. People always say, "If you want a good man, you've got to go to church to find him." Well, if you want a poor to middle class "good man," go to church. Most men who go to church regularly are family men-married, with strong traditional values. Single guys generally don't go to church, at least not single straight guys. Rich guys rarely go to church, unless they're married. You'd be hard pressed to see a single, straight, rich guy in church. That's almost impossible. As a matter of fact, the only rich guy in church is the preacher. So church guys by and large are not good targets. They might make decent marriage material, but for the gold digger, they're to be avoided.

Remember, when you turn any of these guys down, you don't want to reject them in a mean, condescending way. You want to do it very politely. Just dismiss yourself from the situation. You can play it off with, "Hey, I'm married," or "I'm here with someone." You don't want to develop a reputation for being a bitch. There are women out there who are cold and calculating, who consider themselves true gold diggers. You don't have to play the game that way. Everything you want to do has to be done with class. You want to be cool and respectful in everything you do. That's how a true to the game gold digger operates. That's the *only* way a true to the game gold digger operates.

## Gold Digger CHECK LIST #5

### TOP 5 ACCESSORIES A GOLD DIGGER SHOULD NOT HAVE

1. TONGUE RINGS
2. GAUDY TATTOOS
3. BOOTLEG DESIGNER BAGS
4. CUBIC ZIRCONIUM JEWELRY
5. DESIGNER "COKE" SPOON OR CUSTOMIZED WEED PIPE

"SUCCESS IS A GREAT DEODORANT.
IT TAKES AWAY ALL YOUR PAST SMELLS."

— ELIZABETH TAYLOR

# *Chapter Six*

## GOLD DIGGING TOOLS

Now, before you step into the gold digging arena, you will have to prepare yourself psychologically and mentally. The world of gold digging requires you to be disciplined and highly intuitive. I can teach you all kinds of different techniques on what to do and what to say, but if you don't have a certain perception and state of mind about yourself and who you are in the first place, the game won't work. In this chapter, we're going to focus on getting into the mindset of a gold digger. In order to have that mindset, you're going to have to embody ten psychological and mental tools to be a thorough, capable gold digger.

**Gold Digging Tool # 1:**

**Your vocabulary**

To be a good gold digger, you have to expand your mind. You should be well read, for the most part. At the very least, you have to be able to engage in decent but stimulating conversation. One of the best ways you can expand your vocabulary is by reading different books on different subjects. Set a goal for yourself to read at least a book a month. The books don't have to be on astrophysics or advanced oceanography. They could be on almost anything. You don't have to go too deep. On that note, try to avoid trashy, sleazy romantic novels, more affectionately known as chick-lit. While they might provide you some entertainment, they'll do little to enrich your mind. Remember, the object of this tool is to expand your vocabulary through reading. You could start off by checking out the bestsellers-fiction and non-fiction-at your neighborhood bookstore.

Biographies and memoirs are excellent choices in the non-fiction arena, for example. Of course, having a good vocabulary doesn't mean running your mouth all the time. You don't want to be a chatterbox when you get around wealthy men because that's a turnoff. More than that, when you try to use your newfound vocabulary that way, you show how little you actually know.

The reason you want to increase your vocabulary is that when you do meet a rich guy and engage in conversation with him, you can be verbally on par with him. You won't seem out of his league when you talk to him. There's a balance between coming across as intelligent and having an intelligent conversation, and being a person who acts like they know it all. You don't want to be a know-it-all. You use your vocabulary selectively, strategically. To come across as a sexy, sophisticated, and intelligent woman, your vocabulary is very, very important in the gold digging game.

## Gold Digging Tool # 2:
## Good Improv Skills

To be a good gold digger, you have to have good improvisational skills. You have to learn to be very quick on your toes, and very spontaneous. You have to be able to come back with quick nuggets of knowledge and even quicker answers. You don't want to ever seem like you're lost. A good gold digger knows how to adapt to any surrounding. A good gold digger knows how to adapt to any man. When you deal with different targets, they're going to come at you from different directions, in all sorts of different ways. You'll have to be able to adapt to the game that the guy is using towards you. You have to be able to adapt to the

THE ART OF GOLD DIGGING

men who you are targeting. You've got to be quick thinking, but more important, you've got to be quick-witted.

## Gold Digging Tool # 3 :

### A Positive Attitude

I cannot stress this tool often enough. It is very important to speak highly of people. It is very important to have a positive outlook about life, about everything. When you're engaged in conversation with your target, you don't want to come across as a killjoy. You don't want to project a negative aura. When people see that, they lose interest in you. If you have something negative to say about every little thing, you'll be a major turnoff to wealthy men, let alone men in general.

Wealthy men are generally positive in their character makeup. They conduct business in large part by being charismatic and impressing others. Often they want a woman who's the same way. They want a woman who can maintain that same, positive, happy-go-lucky attitude that will only enhance their own positive, happy-go-lucky attitude. A woman like that is infectious with people. People want to be around a woman who has a good vibe and good energy.

You want to at least appear to be as positive as possible. You want to be able to look at everything positively, to be able to see the lighter side of any given situation. That's the image that you want to project when you get around wealthy men.

### Gold Digging Tool # 4 :
### Tactfulness

Tactfulness is a very underrated characteristic in social behavior. There is a right place and a wrong place, a right time and a wrong time, and a right way and a wrong way to do everything. This is very important to know in the gold digging game. Tactfulness is a very underestimated and underappreciated tool. Many of us try to hide behind the guise of being 'real,' or 'keeping it real.' However, there's a difference between keeping it real and being rude. You don't want to say anything that's going to be construed as offensive. You don't want to exude a belligerent or obnoxious persona. Like I said, there's a right way and a wrong way to do anything. You want to be tactful with your words and actions. You don't want to get drunk or high and start screaming inappropriate things at the top of your lungs. You don't want to use excessive profanity in your everyday speech, simply because you won't be thought of as ladylike.

You, as a gold digger, should always come across as a lady, and a classy one at that. There's also a time to be a damsel in distress, and a time to flaunt your intelligence. There's a fine line between those two. Depending on where you are and the rich male company you're keeping, there are times you'll want to play the ditzy damsel role. Many wealthy men are drawn to the damsel in distress. They like a woman they can teach some things to. Of course, you don't want to come off as a complete idiot, but when your target is trying to enlighten you on something, you want to show that you appreciate and respect him. Sometimes playing the coy, cute, dingy role is a real turn-on to certain wealthy guys. You don't want to play too dumb, but being ditzy in a subtle way works countless times. It's no wonder why men are drawn to the Paris Hiltons and Lindsay Lohans and the Jessica Simpsons of the world. These women play up that dingy, damsel-in-distress role. Again, you have to play it in a tactful, subtle way. You don't want to come across as being a moron or an idiot. So always be tactful and appropriate with your actions.

## Gold Digging Tool # 5:
## Confidence

Confidence is one of the most important tools to have. Confidence is really about trusting yourself. Confidence is about having the trust in yourself that you're going to do the best you can do. And more important, you're going to do what you perceive is the right thing. If you have that mentality you will always have a certain level of confidence.

That's what confidence is. It's really trust. Self-confidence equals self-trust. The reason why you're confident in other people is because in large part you trust them. You have confidence in your politicians, doctors, pastors, teachers, etc., because you trust that they're going to be sincere in what they say and in what they do. You trust that they're going to follow through and stay true to their word. You have to embody the same ideology about yourself. You have to know that whatever you do you're going to put in one hundred percent and you're going to be the best you can possibly be. If you win, that's great. If you fail, at least you realize you did the best you could. You're not going to beat yourself up about it. That's confidence. You're going to know that no matter what you are a person of integrity, a person of principle, and a person of intelligence. Internalizing that type of ideology is really going to help you with your confidence.

**Gold Digging Tool # 6:**

**Respect For The Game**

You have to have a genuine respect for the gold digging game in order to be good at it. Too many ladies try to get into situations simply for the outcome-for the money, for the fame, or for the gratitude. You have to be in the gold digging game because you like the rules and sport of the game. You have to be in the gold digging game because in a sense, you're part of a fraternity, or in this case, a sorority. It's your own world. To be a good gold digger, you have to respect what you do. If I could compare being a good gold digger to anything else, it's like being a good basketball player. A lot of basketball players get a lot of money but the really good ones really like the respect of the game. They like the rules of the game. They like the camaraderie of being around other players. They like the science of the sport. As a gold digger in a similar sport, you have to think the same way. You have to like what you do. You have to be addicted to the thrill of the hustle, so to speak. All of this will make you a very, very successful gold digger.

### Gold Digging Tool # 7:

### Upscale Fashion Sense

Keeping your gear on point in the gold digging game is very important. Again, there's a thin line between sexy and slutty. You have to know how to dress in a classy yet seductive way. When you pick your clothes, it's all about the *quality* of your clothes. You don't want to get gaudy clothes. You don't want to get clothes that scream out, "Hey look at me! Look at me! Look at me!" Everything should be elegant, classy, and by all means, sexy. Of course, in the beginning, you'll have to actually buy your own clothes. Try looking into some of the outlet stores in your area. There, you can easily find designer label and other fashion forward clothing that'll be sure to catch a wealthy target's attention. Another alternative that ladies have utilized are some of the resale shops that sell dresses and formal gowns previously worn by celebrities. If you don't mind "gently used," you can find an excellent bargain in an elegant, European-designed outfit.

As an upwardly mobile gold digger, you've also got to step your shoe game up. You don't necessarily have to be like the women in Sex and the City who are literally head over heels obsessed with shoes. At the very least, you want to be into shoes. Wealthy men do look at women's shoes. Wealthy men do look at the style of shoe a woman is wearing. They notice that about women. More than that, shoes and feet are an aphrodisiac to men. Shoes also say a lot about your personality and your sense of style. They say something about your financial situation. When wealthy men see that you have nice shoes, it tells them that you take time out to take care of your feet. If you can take time out and really take good care in making your feet look good by having your footwear look good, that means you're going to take that same care and dedication with other parts of your body and by extension, with other people. That's the subconscious correlation men will make from that.

Someone might invite you to a formal event, and you have to dress a certain way. If you aren't used to dressing up in fancy clothes, and if you're especially uncomfortable wearing heels, wealthy men can tell when you're uncomfortable. When rich men see women in heels, they zone in on the way they walk, and how graceful their stride is. If they see someone teetering like she's about to fall, chances are she'll be out of luck.

Learning how to walk in heels is very, very important. Because you never know when you have to throw some heels on. You have to be able to throw on your heels at the drop of a diamond. You ought to keep a pair in the trunk of your car. Heels scream sophistication. Again, there's a thin line between skanky and sophisticated. That's why you have to learn how to walk in heels. A lot of people who coach models say the best way to walk in high-heeled shoes without them hurting your feet is to walk one foot in front of the other. That will help alleviate the pain and it will give you a graceful, sophisticated look. That will help you look more thorough in the game.

Again, along with the proper shoes, you've got to have an upscale sense of fashion. You don't want to have a swap meet/flea market look. You can't get upscale men looking like you're on a flea market budget. Just because some rich men dress like they stepped out of a flea market, doesn't mean you should too. Bottom line: The target you're after isn't cheap. You have to look the part. If you want to live in a castle, you have to look like a princess.

**Gold Digging Tool # 8:**

**Worldliness**

I know I've said this about other tools, ladies, but worldliness is very important. You have to travel as much as you can. Travel on your own or travel with your friends. You have to get out there and see places, go places and deal with different cultures and different societies. Travel in and around the states. Go to historic points of interest. Check out life in different parts of the country. Ideally, if you can, travel outside the country. Learn a language or two, or at least make a concerted effort in that direction. Learn about different things, so when you do come in contact with wealthy men, you can develop a real sense of camaraderie with them. You might even come in contact with some of these globetrotting guys while traveling. You can build a rapport by talking to them about the different places you've gone to. Traveling is always an excellent icebreaker and conversation starter when it comes to meeting and dealing with men of means. When you talk to them, and you establish that you know where they're from or that you've been where they've been, you now have something in common and you can build from that. Wealthy men are genuinely impressed with a woman who knows her way around the world. A sense of worldliness is very important in the gold digging game.

## Gold Digging Tool # 9:

## A Perceived Sense Of Compassion

Having a sense of compassion about the world is always a positive attribute to have. And even if you are the kind of person who could really care less about anyone or anything besides yourself, you should at least have a *perceived* sense of compassion. It is almost like having a positive attitude, but it's on the next level in the game. By having a perceived sense of compassion, you appear as though you care about different events around the world or about different things in the environment. You have to seem like you care about global warming and endangered species. You have to come across as if you care about the homeless. Again, you have to be perceived as having a sense of compassion. Even if you give less than a damn about the whales or the dolphins or the birds, you have to at least give the impression that you have compassion because this will lower your target's defenses.

When rich men are around new women, many of their defense mechanisms go up. They don't know if the women are there for their money. They're used to dealing with ruthless people all the time, so you have to appear to be as non-threatening and innocent as possible. Your goal is to bring their defenses down. Having that perceived sense of compassion gives you that aura of innocence. There's nothing like the lure of an attractive woman talking about the plight of the defenseless harp seal, or safe drinking water for children. Having that perceived sense of compassion is a very important tool to have.

### Gold Digging Tool # 10:
### A Sense Of Self Discipline

You have to have self-discipline if you want to be a thorough gold digger. Self-discipline is a sign of strength. When you have self-discipline, you'll be able to control your actions with good judgment. When you have a sense of discipline, you will be able to control your actions and not let your actions control you. You will be able to control your emotions and not let your emotions control you. Having self-discipline is extremely important. You don't want to go out with a guy and have a desire to sleep with him on the first date. You'll be throwing self-discipline out the window. At this point, you'll be labeled a slut. Your gold digging tactics will be thrown out the window as well. You've got to be very disciplined when it comes to dealing with your targets, because they're going to try to impress you, they're going to wine and dine you. They're also going to test you and see how weak you are, they're going to try to see what moves and motivates you, they're working really hard to see your Achilles' heel.

You're going to have to stand strong and not be swayed by any of the wealth you see before you. You can't be thrown off your game by any sexual chemistry you and your target may both have. You have to stay on your game and focused on what you need to be focused on-in this case, getting money. Like I said before, wealthy men like the challenge. If you can show that you can go toe to toe with the best of them without breaking down or giving in, the payoff will be worth it. Self-discipline is not only a very important tool of the gold digging game-it is probably the most important. This tool, more than most of the others, will reap immediate rewards.

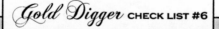

*Gold Digger* CHECK LIST #6

| **TOP 5 SHOES FOR GOLD DIGGERS** | 1. JIMMY CHOO<br>2. MANOLO BLAHNIK<br>3. FERRAGAMO | 4. ROGER VIVIER<br>5. ESCADA |
|---|---|---|

"CHARM IS A WOMAN'S STRENGTH
JUST AS STRENGTH IS A MAN'S CHARM."

— HAVELOCK ELLIS

# Chapter Seven

## WHERE GOLD DIGGERS HANG OUT: PLACES TO MEET TARGETS

Now that you have learned the basic tools of the gold digging game, you need to know where to go to use the tools and the knowledge that you have. There are many places that a true gold digger will hang out at to meet rich men. In all honesty, if you know how to look and what to look for, you can meet rich men almost anywhere. But the following places will give you a good start in your search for a suitable target.

**Golf Courses**

One of the most popular spots to hang out at is the golf course. While many men in general play golf, rich men in particular love to play golf. They play it not just for the love of the game, but as a great networking tool. If you're a woman who wants to learn how to play golf- or, at the very least, look like you want to learn-the golf course is going to be one of your best bets. When you get out there on the green, you can have the whole damsel-in-distress thing going on, and wealthy men will be glad to show you and teach you how to play golf. They love helping a little lady learn the ropes of the game. This is also a great opportunity for a conversation starter as well. If you want to be a good gold digger, definitely take up golf.

**Upscale Gyms and Health Spas**

Another place that attracts wealthy men is a private, upscale gym, located in a more exclusive part of town. Now here's a place where you not only can meet a man of means, you can see him doing something he really enjoys doing. There are plenty of wealthy men who love working out. They love staying in shape. They love having their look together. They love feeling disciplined and doing their thing. Men of this caliber also want their women to be healthy and in shape. For you, a disciplined and healthy gold digger, meeting a man this way can be ideal.

## Upscale Sporting Good Stores

Speaking of sports and physical activity, an upscale sporting goods store is another place you can go to find wealthy guys. Like I said, rich men love to work out and they love to be physically active. But they also love to check out upscale sporting goods stores. They love to buy the latest equipment and supplies to take care of their bodies. Whether it's the most advanced ski gear money could buy, high tech camping or climbing accessories, rich men know what they want. Show up at one of these stores, and you'll only enhance their "shopping" experience.

## Upscale Hair Salons

Another excellent place where you can meet rich men is an upscale hair salon. A lot of rich guys love to get their hair cut, trimmed and styled. You always see these rich guys with their hair looking perfect. Most upscale hair salons tend to be unisex, that is, cater to both men and women. Find out which ones are unisex, and plan to go to one of these establishments in your town-if it's sophisticated enough, or better yet-a nearby city. Make an appointment to go in there to get your nails done. Most of these salons have manicurists and other services on the premises as well. You might not only find a wealthy target, but one whose guard is down.

### High End Shoe Stores

Now, another place you can meet upscale, rich men is a high-end shoe store. Rich men love to get shoes for themselves. They love to wear quality shoes. You can go to an upscale, Kenneth Cole store for example. Go in there like you're looking for shoes for your uncle or for your dad. If you see a wealthy-looking gentleman there, you can strike up a conversation with him. You can be cute and courteous and ask, "Excuse me, I'm trying to buy some shoes for my uncle, because we're having a special event," or, "It's my uncle's wedding anniversary, and I wanted to know, in your opinion, what would be a good pair of shoes to get him?" You can ask something subtle like this to start up a conversation to kind of break the ice. In this shopping environment, you can turn the tables and ask him for help. Odds are, he'll be more than happy to accommodate. So upscale shoe stores are a good bet.

### Dog Parks

Another place you can meet wealthy guys is at a dog park in a wealthy neighborhood in your city. Many wealthy guys have dogs, especially well-pedigreed varieties. They enjoy walking and showing off their dogs. They also take the time to take care and spoil their dogs. Depending where you are, you can find many well-to-do men at a dog park. And that's a good place to strike up a conversation and break the ice. As an extension of this, walking a dog in an upscale neighborhood is another good way for you to meet wealthy guys. Even walking around in places like Beverly Hills, Palm Beach, or the Hamptons with your dog, you'll most likely see someone wealthy walking their dog. You might decide to run into them and strike up a conversation that way. If you live near the beach, walking your dog in a nice, upscale stretch is another way to meet wealthy men. If you don't have your own dog, borrow one from a friend. Also, go to pet stores in upscale neighborhoods as well. Here you will easily bump into wealthy men buying food and supplies for their dogs.

**Jogging In Wealthy Neighborhoods**

If you don't have a pet, you ought to go bike riding or jogging in a wealthy neighborhood. A nice stretch of beach works just as well. These are good alternatives, primarily so you can have contact with the people in that area. If you're in So Cal, jog in Malibu or along the outlying areas of Beverly Hills such as Bel Air or Holmby Hills. If you're up in New York, try the Hamptons. In Florida, Miami and Palm Beach obviously come to mind. These are but a few places where you can strike up a conversation with somebody. Places where you can interact and mingle with upscale people. There are many other places-too many to list. No matter where you live, you'll surely be able to find a nice, affluent neighborhood to jog or ride your bike in.

On a side note, in many of these places you won't even have to strike up the conversation yourself. Just by positioning yourself in these locations, many guys will simply step to you. It's really about timing. It's all about positioning yourself strategically in the right locations. Just getting to a spot and being in the right place at the right time, that's about eighty percent of the game right there. The rest should fall into place.

**Bookstores**

A place where you can meet wealthy men is the bookstore. Bookstores are very popular. But most wannabe gold diggers will avoid them. You can definitely meet wealthy dudes at the bookstore. Many of them read voraciously, and gain a higher level of education in the process. They tend to go to bookstores in nice areas in the cities where you live. I emphasize 'nice areas,' because if you're in a part of town that's considered middle class or lower middle class-usually a suburb-and you're in a bookstore, you'll mostly find students and college kids. In other words, guys who don't have a lot of money. You really have to go to an upscale part of town to meet the rich, book worm.

## High End Grocery Stores

Another great place to meet wealthy men are high-end grocery stores like Trader Joe's and Whole Foods Market. Many wealthy men love to eat healthy. They especially love to eat organic food. Trader Joe's and Whole Foods are loaded with wealthy people. The food items there are a little more expensive than at a regular grocery store, but to wealthy men, their health has no price tag. If you can't afford to shop there on a regular basis, check it out at the very least. You're sure to find something that you can't get anywhere else. Check out the vitamin section, and when you see a wealthy guy, ask him questions. He'll be happy you did.

## Exotic Racecar Events

A racecar event is an excellent place to meet wealthy guys. A lot of folks don't know about this. And when I say racecar event, I don't mean Nascar. Nascar is supported largely by working class, blue-collar people. Unfortunately, it continues to have a hillbilly aura surrounding it. The only wealthy dudes involved with Nascar are the drivers, crew chiefs, and owners. When I say racecar event, I'm talking about an exotic car event. I'm talking Ferraris, Lamborghinis, and Porsches, and the men who race them. Many wealthy men hang out at places like this, because they love expensive, high performance cars. In order to participate at an exotic car event, one has to have serious money to have a car to get into one of these races. For wealthy men, it's like a hobby to them. Women don't generally know about this. This is a great little secret of the gold digging game. Many rich guys-including celebrities-participate at these exclusive events. It's a good way for them to mingle and network chop up game with each other.

One more type of racecar event that wealthy people attend is the Formula or F-1 racing event. The Indy 500, the Grand Prix, and the 24 Hours of Le Mans are but a few notable races. Only large corporations or wealthy individuals can own one of these cars. Some celebrities, like the late Paul Newman, not only involve themselves in the ownership of some of these cars, they also race them. If you can get to one of these events, you'll be able to mingle with some prominent, world-renowned racecar drivers, corporate bosses, and other influential men of means.

**Boat Shows**

Another place to meet wealthy guys is at a boat show. Boat shows are very important, because again, in order to have a boat, you need money. Now, I'm not talking about those eight-foot inflatable rafts you played in when you were a kid. I'm talking about those fifty foot-and bigger-motor or sailing boats you see at a show. In other words, yachts. When wealthy guys own one of these boats, they like to show it off. They like to participate in boating events. It's not surprising that these events are loaded with wealthy guys. And most events by the water are pretty good places to meet them. Along with these boat show events, you want to consider yacht clubs as well. Wealthy men hang out there like a second home.

To get into one of these exclusive establishments, you have to either be a member or a guest of one. If you play your cards right, it shouldn't take long for you to get into one of these clubs. Don't confuse boating guys with surfers guys. A lot of these men have good character, but they generally have no money. So when I say go for targets at water events, I'm definitely not referring to beach bums and broke surfer dudes. You want to try to avoid the surfers altogether. You want to go for the guys who own and run the big boats, guys who are into some serious water sport vehicles. On a related note, you might want to stay away from boat owners who live on their boats full time. These guys are usually retired and they have nothing else to do, but talk about boating and water. You will get bored with that very quickly.

### Charity Events

A charity event is a perfect place to meet wealthy guys. It's a great place to see wealthy guys who are ready to donate money. When you are at a charity event, just being there makes you seem like a person who cares about the cause. That's a good look on you. It makes you come across as a very sensitive, unselfish person. That's the vibe that you want to have. That's the vibe you want to project. You always want to have a very innocent, wholesome vibe about yourself. Nothing could be more innocent and wholesome than you donating your time at an event to benefit and help somebody else, or even appearing to be donating your time. Just make sure to pick a charity event that will have a high profile. An event that will attract the city's wealthy and popular. Again, charity events are great places to meet wealthy men.

### Upscale Hotels

Happy hour at an upscale hotel is another great place to meet wealthy men. Every city has at least one or two upscale hotels. There are cities with several upscale hotels. You can go there during happy hour, either alone or with a friend, just to wind down and have a drink. There may be wealthy businessmen in town who may be there to wind down themselves and mingle with the right company. The hotel bar is a great place to rub elbows with the upper crust in your neighborhood or city. For example, out here in Los Angeles, there are many fine hotels in Beverly Hills, in Brentwood, and in Hollywood. People come here to do business and handle things. This is a great environment to do your thing. There are fine hotel bars in other major cities as well. Miami, Dallas, and New York stand out. Even if a wealthy guy is a light drinker, at a bar he will tend to drop some of his inhibitions, which will make better game for you.

**The Internet**

Another place to meet wealthy guys is the good old, tried and true Internet. The Internet is home to many networking places. You can do just about everything on the Internet. Back in the day, it was regarded as taboo to meet somebody on the Internet because it was considered to be so impersonal. Being on a matchmaker site had a certain negative stigma attached to it. Now, though, it's more accepted. You can shop for food and clothes, pay bills-just about everything is at your fingertips. Nowadays, it's natural to meet people and mingle on the Internet. There's nothing wrong with that. Myspace and Facebook are cool and popular web destinations for meeting people, but there are other websites that cater specifically to the gold digging crowd. One website is called wealthymen.com. Another, appropriately called sugardaddyforme.com, is a site where you can go in, create a simple profile and mingle with wealthy men who want to meet attractive "sugar babies," so to speak. The Internet is definitely a good place to meet wealthy gentlemen. In the long run, there's no substitute for the real thing, but the Internet is a great start.

**Best Cities For Gold Digging**

Now, there are cities that are particularly suited for gold diggers. It's a given the gold digging game can work anywhere in the world. However, here in the States, the top five cities for gold diggers are Los Angeles, New York, Miami, Atlanta, and Dallas. Although wealthy men live everywhere on the planet, they seem to congregate in these particular places. As a gold digger looking for a wealthy man, your chances increase in these five cities. In Los Angeles, you have the Hollywood new money, there's plenty of old money in New York, in Miami, there's a lot of both. Miami is a beautiful place as well. Many wealthy businessmen flock to Atlanta. Dallas is a well-known hotspot for rich people as well.

A good city to get started and practice your game in is Vegas. Las Vegas is a great practice spot-and I say practice spot because it's not a good place to live in long term to really utilize your game. This is because, for better or worse, Vegas is still known as a one night stand type of town. There are people in and out every single day. There's also the whole vibe of "Whatever happens in Vegas stays in Vegas." As a gold digger, you want to keep getting your money after you leave. Vegas is a good spot to at least test your game out. You can do some quick interactions with people and feel them out. It's always wise for a good player to practice her game, no matter how good she is. Las Vegas is probably the best place to get a taste of the gold digging game on a short term basis.

## Meeting Targets While On Vacation

When you take a trip or go on vacation, you can meet ideal targets. If you're in Hawaii, Jamaica, France, Greece-just about any resort destination around the world-they are all good places to vibe and interact with wealthy targets. Most wealthy men love to travel. They love to travel in style and luxury. When you're on vacation, if you meet a guy from the country or city you're from, there's a very good chance he might be wealthy. It takes serious money to travel around the world. Taking a trip is a good way to really build your gold digger portfolio. Like I said before, traveling gives you conversation material when you meet people. It gives you something in common with wealthy men. When you go on vacation, think about the number of wealthy men who've also been to the same places you've been to. You now have something in common to talk about. Vacation spots are excellent places to meet wealthy men.

On a side note regarding vacations, going on trips with your target can be a very tricky situation. Many times when a woman meets a target, the target may offer to take the woman on a vacation. Now, remember, you as a good gold digger have to be very careful about how you interact sexually with your targets. Because when you just meet a guy, and he wants to immediately take you on a vacation within the first few days of knowing you, that should send you a red flag. Usually, a guy like this wants to get you out of your element. In other words, he wants to get you to have sex with him. He knows that once you're away from what's familiar to you, you're going to be a little more vulnerable. Your guard will be down, simply because you're in a strange place. You don't have your network of friends to support you and talk you out of things.

As I've said before, in the gold digging game, you don't want to have sex too soon because the minute you do, you don't have anything left to bargain with. You don't want to put yourself out there like that. Here's a tip: When you go on vacation with a target immediately after meeting him, you have to dust off the old school, "It's that time of the month" line, if you know what I mean. Although it is an old trick, it continues to work, time and time again. What you do is buy a big box of tampons before the trip, and make it obvious. At the same time, you want to exercise a certain amount of subtlety. When you get to your destination, you can use that as your excuse. You can say that you want to "do it" and "take it to the next level," but that you can't for the reason I just indicated. The bottom line, you do not want to flat-out reject your target because that will leave a negative vibe. You want to be able to do it in such a way that your target will come back wanting you more. Remember: As a true to the game gold digger, you've got to be subtle in the way you do things.

*Gold Digger* CHECK LIST #7

## TOP 5 CLUBS AND BARS AROUND THE WORLD FOR GOLD DIGGERS TO HANG OUT

1. NIKKI BEACH RESTAURANT/BAR IN ST. TROPEZ, FRANCE
2. THE BELLAGIO HOTEL IN LAS VEGAS, NV.
3. THE LAPIDUS BAR IN SOUTH BEACH MIAMI, FL.
4. THE LEFT BANK RESTAURANT/BAR IN DUBAI
5. MR. CHOW'S RESTAURANT/BAR IN BEVERLY HILLS, CA.

"WOMEN ARE PERFECTLY WELL AWARE
THAT THE MORE THEY SEEM TO OBEY
THE MORE THEY RULE."


— JULES MICHELET

# Chapter Eight

## RULES OF THE GOLD DIGGING GAME

In any game you participate in, there has to be rules. There has to be order. There has to be some type of protocol to follow in order to be successful or in order to maintain the integrity of the game you're playing. In the gold digging game, there are certain rules that you have to administer upon yourself. These rules will help you maintain your standards. These rules will help you have a sense of integrity when you're dealing with your targets. You will live by these rules in the gold digging game.

Now, according to the Wikipedia dictionary, integrity is the basing of one's actions on an internally consistent framework of principles. To translate that into what you as a gold digger can use, the basic definition of integrity is having self-imposed rules and standards that you live by.

The bottom line: If you don't have integrity, you won't be taken seriously, let alone be able to perform as a gold digger on top of her game.

### Rule # 1:

### Establish Your Importance Early

When dealing with men, you end how you start. Establish early on that your target should roll out the red carpet for you. That's very important, ladies. When you meet a wealthy guy, you have to let him know right away that he has to do things for you. You do this simply by carrying yourself in such a way that he will instinctively respond to your bidding. He has to know that you are a high maintenance young lady. If you come across as low budget, he's going to treat you like you're low budget. You have to establish yourself early on the way you want to be treated. There is nothing like first impressions. Wealthy guys are going to test you. Some of these targets are going to try to play you like you're beneath them. You have to step up to the plate and let them know that you're high maintenance and that they'll have to continue to treat you like you're high maintenance. You've got to look the look, walk the walk, and last but not least, talk the talk in order for your target to roll it out for you in the gold digging game.

### Rule # 2:

### Learn How To Value Your Time

People in general like to waste time and mess around because they have a lot of idle time and have nothing better to do. Some even waste others' time and think nothing of it. As a true to the game gold digger, you must always utilize your time wisely. Even if you have to pick up a hobby or two, you've got to do something. There's an old saying, "An idle mind is the devil's workshop." When you have nothing constructive to do, your mind automatically shifts into negativity.

To avoid this, you want to keep your mind and your time occupied. If you notice , people with nothing better to do tend to nitpick and become gossipy, bickering about minute things. They engage in petty things and petty conversation. They engage in negative habits and negative behaviors. As a true to the game gold digger, you've got to be larger than this. You've got to be above gossip, b.s. and petty things. You have better things in your life to do. A true gold digger isn't going to sit around gossiping about Brangelina, Katie and Tom, JayZ and Beyonce, or where is Mariah Carey vacationing. You are not going to be chitchatting about any of that because you are going to be the one on vacation, you are going to be the one traveling the world, you are going to be the one living the lavish life yourself. You won't have time to talk about somebody else living that lifestyle. But in order to attain that lifestyle, you have to stay active on a daily basis in everything you do. You've got to keep busy to stay on top of your game.

### Rule # 3:

### Never *Blatantly* Reject Your Target

When you meet a wealthy guy, or a guy in general, and they're not up to par or you're not feeling their vibe, you never want to reject them in a nasty, distasteful way. Even when you're dealing with a target and he's making strong advances towards you, you need to gently turn him down or deflect him in a very smooth, subtle way. You can laugh things off, giggle about stuff, even give him a mild brush-off, but you never want to blatantly turn your target down.

Let's say a target wants you to spend the night with him at his home. You never want to say, "Hell no, I'd never do that." You never want to diss the gentleman. You want to play it real cool. For example, you can say something like, "I have to respectfully decline." Again, you have to be very cool about it. The reason why you don't want to blatantly reject targets is because a lot of these guys think with their egos. As a gold digger, you want to cater to and stroke their egos. You want to make them feel manly. At the same time, however, you never want to be considered a doormat. You definitely don't want to come across as a bitch. There's a fine line between being a doormat and a bitch, a line between coming across as too sweet and subtle, and aggressive and hard. You want to be right there in that lukewarm, middle position, where you can deflect them. No matter how smoothly and subtly you work it, you want to be stern and still get your point across.

**Rule # 4:**

**Always Come Across As Being Unattainable**

You want your target to pursue you. You want to have your target earn you. You want your target to court you. The reason is a simple one: People value what they work for. They value something that they have to chase. If you go to a restaurant and they're giving away free food, you don't value that food. You look at that situation and think the restaurant must be desperate because they're giving away free samples. Likewise, if you go to a supermarket and they're giving away free samples, and you eat free food-even if the food is great-you just don't place the same value to it. But if you go to a restaurant and the food is a hundred dollars a plate, psychologically you're going to think that the food is better. Even if the food ends up being mediocre or tasting bland, psychologically you're going to think the food is better because it's more high-priced.

You're going to think that the food is of a better quality, regardless of the outcome. You want to have that kind of mentality as a gold digger. You want to seem like a prize-which you are-if you're internalizing the game in this book. You're learning how to tap into the prize within you. Again, you want to come across as being unattainable, like you're not quite ready for a serious relationship. You have to be courted into a relationship, slowly, gradually. Your time is such where you seem a little too busy to spend with your target. You always want to keep your target chasing.

**Rule # 5:**

**Never Take Food To Go From Restaurants**

When you go out on dates with a target, never, ever take food to go at a restaurant. This is a mistake many if not most women make. When ladies go to a nice restaurant, enjoy their meal and hear the waiter say,

" Would you like to take some food to go?" not used to being in a nice restaurant, they may reply, "Oh, yes, I'll take something to go!" Next thing you know, they're getting doggie bags and taking them out of the restaurant. That's the worst thing a gold digger can do. That looks very cheap and tacky. Targets won't necessarily say that, but that truly looks cheap on your part. In this context, "take out" should never be in a gold digger's vocabulary. Never, ever take food to go. That makes you look like you're not used to eating at nice places. That kind of behavior is acceptable with your girlfriends, but never with targets. Carrying around a doggy bag gives you a peasant-like, cheap date, buffet type of vibe. You never want to have that type of vibe. Again, never take food to go at a restaurant when you are trying to make a good impression with a wealthy target. Ever.

### Rule # 6 :

### Always Let Your Target Know That You Have Options

You never want to seem like your target is doing you a favor by trying to date you. You should always appear to be in demand even if you are not in demand. You want to let your target know in a subtle way that you have other options besides spending time with him. You don't have to be with him. You don't have to be up under him. You have hobbies that you can get into. You have other girlfriends who you could be hanging out with. You have other male suitors or male friends you could be going out on dinner dates with , having drinks with or having coffee with. Again, you want to always seem like you have options because people tend to respect people more who have options. People tend to respect people more who have a full social calendar rather than endless nights spent in front of the TV. Options are very, very important to have in the gold digging game.

**Rule # 7:**

**Invest In Yourself**

You really have to invest in yourself first. There's an old saying that goes, "It takes money to make money." That's very true. Sometimes you have to splurge on nice outfits. Sometimes you have to splurge on nice boots. You have to splurge on getting your hair fly. That's one of the perks of the gold digging game. And every now and then you might have to splurge to get your look looking the way you need and want to look. You have to have quality gear. You have to make yourself look like a million bucks if you're trying to attract a million bucks. You can't get Rodeo Drive men with the swap meet look. That's very important to understand. You can't have a low budget look trying to get wealthy men. You really have to invest in yourself. And when your targets see that you invest in yourself and take care of yourself, they're going to want to continue the process as well. They'll say to themselves, "This woman is taking care of herself, and she's looking good, and she's going to the nice stores, and she dresses nice, I have to step to her a certain way."

If you treat yourself right by investing in yourself, other people will treat you right and invest in you as well. As I mentioned before in an earlier chapter, you can always make the initial investment in outfits by shopping at outlet stores or resale boutiques. You'll look like money without spending a lot of it. But remember, if you don't invest in yourself, how can you expect a target to do the same?

### Rule # 8:

### Never Become Totally Dependent On Your Target

This is a mistake that countless women make. They get a sugar daddy, who gets them in a position of total dependency. Never let him do that, because that's the modus operandi of a sugar daddy. He wants to get you in a situation where he's paying the rent and car notes, knowing that he can snatch it all away at any given moment. You always want to get things in your name. The reason is simple: Sugar daddies are unpredictable. They can switch up and change their game up any minute. Some of these guys might have a wife you don't know about. Some of them might have a new girlfriend who just popped up into the picture.

Ladies, don't think with your egos, because these guys will sit up and tell you that you're the best thing since sliced bread, only to tell you the next day, "I'm done with you. I've got a new girlfriend." You have to understand how targets think. Always prepare yourself for those "just in case" moments. The most successful gold diggers are those who think independently and logically. They don't rely on anything else, and definitely not on anyone else to take care of things. You want to rely on yourself. Part of the sugar daddy game is they'll offer to get you a nice house, they'll offer to get you a car, or something else of prime importance. Sugar daddies make it all seem like you have them wrapped around your finger. Unfortunately, the opposite is true: They're getting you wrapped around their fingers. That's the trick a lot of women don't know about. Once you get into that house, once you get into that car, you're under their command. Now, they're running the show. They are calling the shots. Remember, a true to the game gold digger is always in control of the game.

## Rule # 9:

### You Are In Control Of All Interactions

Understand that you are in control of all the interactions. You never let the target control the flow. Like I said before, you let him think that he's in control, but you always run the show as a true gold digger. You don't want to be the type of woman who jumps whenever your target says jump. Don't ever let a target manipulate or pressure you into any situation. No matter how much money they give you,never let a target use money to control you.

## Rule # 10:

### You Have To Be Unpredictable At Times

Now, ladies, here's an interesting rule: You have to be unpredictable at times. There's a saying that goes, "familiarity breeds contempt." When people get too used to you, they almost develop a certain level of disdain.

Rich targets like things to be unpredictable. They like adventure. You don't want to become boring. On the contrary, you don't want to be too wild. You don't want to be a drug abusing, attention freak. You don't want to go down that route. But you do want to be unpredictable. You change your patterns every now and then. This could be as simple as switching hobbies. You can rearrange your daily routine. You can change your look. It could be something as subtle as that. If you're used to going to the mall everyday, at the same time of day, think about heading for the gym instead. There are all kinds of little things you can do to switch up the pace and throw your target off-guard. That way, he won't be able to simply put you in a box. Always come across as a little unpredictable. When they think they know you, turn left and go the other way. You always want to keep them on their toes.

It's like putting together a puzzle. When you're working a puzzle, you're intrigued by that puzzle because you're trying to figure it out. Once you put the puzzle together, you're not intrigued anymore. You have it figured out. As a gold digger, you want to keep adding pieces to the puzzle so your target will never fully figure you out. Change your demeanor and attitude. One day, act totally happy-go-lucky. The next day, you have a dead-serious look on your face. Change your game up constantly, and throw your target off-guard. This isn't to say, however, that you want to be flaky. Like in many of the other rules in the art of gold digging, there's a fine line here. You want to be unpredictable, but you do want to show up when you should be showing up. Again, change your game, and make your target meet you at your terms.

**Rule # 11:**

**Do Not Use Excessive Profanity**

Excessive profanity is very unladylike. And it cheapens you. A lot of women will use curse words as adjectives. A few curse words here or there are understandable and even acceptable, because you don't want to seem too uptight. You don't want to come across as a prude. But excessive profanity-where every other word is a curse word-you don't want to do that. It gives you a low-budget look. It also gives you a reputation for coming across as uneducated and ignorant. If you're upset, and you slip a word or two, fine. But you don't want to sound cheap or "just one of the guys." Without exception, a gold digger always carries herself with class.

## Rule # 12:

### Never Give Up Sex On A First Date

A true gold digger would never "do the do" on the first date with a target. The second date is cool. The third date is cool as well. Honestly, in the gold digging game, if you could hold out as long as possible, that's best. But whatever you do, you never want to do it on the first date. When a woman has sex on a first date, in many cases she automatically gets put into a booty call category. Ladies, it is very difficult to get out of the booty call category. Men do not like to invest financially in a booty call. Usually, for a target, sex is the trump card. To better illustrate this, ladies, if you meet a guy, and he's a simp or a pushover, it's hard to view him as anything else. So if he views you as a booty call, it's going to be hard for him to view you as anything else. So you never want to give up sex on the first date.

There's something about the first date or hooking up with a woman and having sex with her. Men tend to put her in a certain category, usually not favorable to her. A man automatically knows in the back of his mind that no matter how much you tell him "Oh, I've never done this before," or "This isn't me," he assumes that if you're doing it with him, you're doing it with everybody else. That doesn't make you seem like a good investment. It makes you seem weak, to say the least. And rich guys don't want to invest in a weak stock. So at least exercise that level of restraint in your actions to be a worthy investment for your target. Again, if you could hold out for as long as possible, that would be ideal.

## Rule # 13:

### Learn How To Play The Humanitarian

I've mentioned this before. You always want to come across as the good Samaritan. Always come across as the environmentalist, or the PETA sympathizer. A lot of rich guys assume that most women out there who try to step to them are selfish. You have to prove otherwise. You have to set the bar. Many women have their hands out, looking to these men to do something for them, to provide something for them. But if you can come across as a selfless humanitarian, or as someone who cares about the environment and what goes on in the world, your target will respect that. It will lower his defenses. That, in turn, will put you on the offense.

### Rule # 14:

### Lower Your Target's Defenses

One of the best ways to lower your target's defenses is to pay for a few dates yourself. Usually, when women go on dates with guys, especially wealthy guys, women expect to be wined and dined. And that's cool. Most wealthy guys expect women to expect that. But again, you being unpredictable, and lowering your target's defenses, every now and then you're going to have to pay for the date yourself. When you do it, you have to do it in a very nonchalant way. Many women will make the mistake of taking the guy out and making it a big, special event. A birthday would be a good example. Valentine's Day and Christmas are others. They make it seem like it's very rare that this is happening. Now, when you take your rich target out on a date, you have to act like it's no big deal. It has to be nonchalant, carefree, and at the same time direct.

The reason you do it like that is when your target sees that you're that nonchalant and carefree about paying for a date and spending a little money on him, he's going to be that nonchalant and carefree about spending money on you. As a matter of fact, he's going to try to up you and do you one better because it might mess with his ego a little bit by having a woman treat him to dinner. That's why he's going to up the stakes-which, ultimately, is exactly what you want.

Also, this is a great way to throw him off the scent of thinking you're after his money. If you're spending your hard-earned cash on him, he will think very highly of you. Be unpredictable, and treat him once in a while. It's a perfect strategy for a true to the game gold digger.

### Rule # 15:

### Wear Lots of White Outfits

If you notice, a lot of wealthy people wear white outfits. Many wealthy people in places like Beverly Hills and The Hamptons often have "white parties", where the patrons are required to come dressed in all white attire. White clothes give off the illusion of wealth and success even if you are not rich. Contrary to popular belief, the tradition of wearing white clothes (especially white wedding dresses) did not initially represent purity and innocence. It represented wealth. In 1840, Queen Victoria married Albert of Saxe, and wore what was then considered a flamboyant white gown. Many women saw this as a statement of class and style, and copied the Queen by also getting married in white. Getting married in a white, extravagant gown was a sign that you could afford to buy a dress that you would never be able to wear again because of its style and color. Back then, it took a lot of labor to create white fabrics (it was also difficult to clean white fabrics- as it is today). And because of this, white fabrics cost more, therefore making it a symbol of status and wealth. And this symbol of status associated with white clothes is still prevalent in the collective consciousness of our culture today. So if it's the right season, try to wear as many white outfits as you can.

*Gold Digger* CHECK LIST #8

## TOP 5 DESIGNER SUNGLASSES FOR GOLD DIGGERS

1. DIOR
2. CHANEL
3. DOLCE & GABBANA
4. VERSACE
5. ROBERTO CAVALLI

"MONEY, IF IT DOES NOT BRING YOU HAPPINESS, WILL AT LEAST HELP YOU BE MISERABLE IN COMFORT."

— HELEN GURLEY BROWN

# Chapter Nine

## THE DIFFERENCE BETWEEN A GOLD DIGGER & A SCAM ARTIST

A true gold digger never causes any kind of harm or detriment to a person in order to get money. A true gold digger never scams, embezzles, swindles, or extorts money from a guy. Whenever you hear news stories about certain women scheming money out of a guy, the media will automatically label them as gold diggers. People viewing or reading the news will assume the worst. The sad reality is, nothing could be further from the truth. These women are not gold diggers. Real gold diggers are hustlers. There's a difference between being a hustler and a scam artist. There's a difference between being a gold digger and a scam artist. A hustler comes up with ways to make money that could be done on a consecutive basis, where the rewards outweigh the risk. A scam artist is a person who doesn't know how to make money on a consecutive basis and the risk outweighs the rewards. A gold digger has integrity. A scam artist does not. If you intend to do any scamming, this is the wrong book for you.

Someone who is a scam artist will make money in a quick, temporary way. For example, a woman might write bad checks and do this for a period of time. Eventually, it all catches up with her and she'll do three to five years in jail for writing bad checks. Someone who's a strong-arm robber will also make money temporarily. He'll go into a store and rob it for eighty dollars. Eventually, he'll get caught and do ten years in prison for that same eighty dollars. That's scamming. That's not hustling. That's the difference between a hustler and a scam artist. A gold digger isn't a scam artist. A gold digger knows you don't have to commit a potential crime in order to get money. People scam when they run out of game. They scam when they have no game to begin with. A true gold digger is always going to have game and stay true to the game. She does not have to resort to causing somebody harm or detriment. If she feels compelled to do this, it's a sign she needs to move on or get out of the gold digging business entirely.

Now ladies, **if you engage in one or more of the five following scams, you are not a true-to-the-game gold digger:**

### # 1: The Pregnancy Scam

Now, most if not all women who get involved with the Pregnancy Scam tend to be incorrectly categorized as gold diggers. What these women do is have sex with as many celebrities or public figures as possible. When they end up getting pregnant by one of these celebrities, they think they'll be on Easy Street collecting money for child support. This has happened a lot with NBA players in particular, especially in the 90s. The League has since cracked down on players having so many kids out of wedlock. During the 90s, this sort of behavior was at an all-time high, where these women were successfully getting the players with the Pregnancy Scam. Though enormously successful, these guys were rather naïve and didn't know the game. In the 90's, a lot of NBA players started to get recruited fresh out of high school or right out of their first year in college. A lot of young, naïve men were becoming millionaires overnight. And these guys were laying up with any and every female who gave them the time of day. These guys were ripe for the picking,because women started preying on them en masse. It had gotten so bad,that in the late 90's, Sports Illustrated did an infamous cover story about the high number paternity suits against many players in the league. This was not a good look for the NBA franchise,and they have since cracked down on athletes engaging in reckless,off-court behavior.

The Pregnancy Scam isn't limited to just athletes. Other areas where celebrities are involved, you'll find women with limited game scamming for their next meal ticket. Take, for example, the actor Robert Blake. A few years ago, woman by the name of Bonnie Lee Blakeley claimed that Robert was the father of her baby. She also claimed that Christian Brando, Marlon Brando's son, was the father. A DNA test proved that Blake was indeed the father. Less than two years later, Bonnie Lee Blakely was found murdered. Whenever you participate in any type of scam,even if it's technically a *legal* scam (the Pregnancy Scam is one of the only scams where you can blatantly lie and not get prosecuted ) there is always the potential for negative or even deadly repercussions. Like I said before,as a gold digger,you never want to put yourself in a potentially negative or dangerous situation.

A true-to-the-game gold digger does not have to give birth to get her money. I personally take issue with the pregnancy scam because there's a third party involved - in this case, a child. The child is always, without question, an innocent victim. Children don't need to be a part of the hustle. Children should never be used as pawns. That's not fair game. That's playing below the belt when you put children in the mix. A true gold digger can use her own verbal skills and integrity to get money without involving a child. A child is oblivious to what's going on. A child is a victim, plain and simple. For a gold digger, getting knocked up to get her money is only going to hinder her abilities to do what she needs to do. Once a gold digger finds the target of her dreams, then and only then she should think of having children.

### #2: The Rape Scam

Now, another scam that some women use is the Rape Scam. We saw how that played out with Kobe Bryant a few years ago. There are a number of women who get with celebrities, have sex with them, and turn around and say they were raped. They'll bring charges and if things go their way, they'll file a civil suit and try to get money from that. That's considered a scam because it only works as a hit or miss thing. It's either going to work once or it's not going to work at all. You can't keep doing the Rape Scam. Either you come up big with it, or when the truth comes out, you're going to lose all credibility. Not surprisingly, that happened with the young lady in the Kobe Bryant case. That has happened with many entertainers who've been excused of rape and sexual misconduct by women trying to make a fast buck. Some women have gotten paid from it; most don't get paid. That's a very low budget, quick buck scam that should never be attributed to gold diggers.

### #3: The Extortion Scam

This particular scam is usually used with married targets. This is the scam in which women have relationships with a celebrity or a certain wealthy man and they threaten to go public with the affair in a negative way. They'll try to extort money from the gentleman to keep his mouth shut. They'll threaten to tell the guy's wife about the affair. If he doesn't give hush money, they'll try to blackmail the target. They'll tell the target they're going to go public with a story about his infidelity or homosexuality or they will start a rumor saying that he has a disease, etc.

There are many types of extortion scams that these women use, but all in all, they usually work on married men. Other types of extortion scams also work on men of power, particularly politicians. Women will have affairs with these guys,then sell information to the tabloids, or the mainstream media. Extortion is just another low budget way to hustle, because that only works one time. You can't have a reputation for embarrassing targets, at least not at this level. This is not something that you can do repeat business with. If it's not a one-time deal, it's definitely a limited pursuit. Regardless of the outcome, you will lose credibility that way. A gold digger would never do something that would only work once.

## # 4 : The Palimony Scam

Palimony is when you are legally obligated provide financial support to a non-marital significant other. The whole palimony phenomenon came into the scene in the 1970s with a very famous Hollywood actor from that time, Lee Marvin. At the time, his live-in girlfriend said that he promised to take care of her, and they ended up going to court over it. In the end, the court reached some type of settlement, although it was a fraction of what she originally sought. Still, the damage was done. It set a precedent for all future palimony seekers. Since that landmark case, countless women have been trying to use the Palimony Scam with wealthy men and celebrities.

More recently, another celebrity, comedian Bill Maher, had a girlfriend who claimed that he would take care of her financially and when they broke up she tried to sue him for palimony money.

Remember, ladies, the palimony thing only works one time. You've got to watch out for that. You cannot keep filing palimony suits. Like most scams, it's a hit or miss situation, and often, it's going to miss. That's not a gold digger's forte to try to sue a wealthy guy for palimony. Either you get money from him directly or you don't. If you don't get money, you move onto the next target. A lot of women try to scam a guy out of palimony money because the target pretty much got over on them. These wannabe gold diggers wasted their time and didn't get their money when they were supposed to be getting their money- which was every day. After the relationship inevitably comes to an end, the target has cut them loose.

Now they want to try to come back and say he owes them palimony. They should have been up on their game to begin with. They should not have been sitting up there letting the target tell them all these things and take it all passively. They should have let it go in one ear and out the other. Women who get involved in these types of scams do it out of anger and out of frustration for not getting the money they were supposed to get in the first place.

### #5: The Cat Burglar Scam

Now, the fifth scam is the Cat Burglar Scam. You have women who will get around rich men and celebrities and literally steal from them. They'll sneak into the guy's wallet. They'll steal jewelry from them. They'll steal important documents and other personal items. Women like this will even set up rich men to be robbed by other men. The Cat Burglar Scam is a major scam that will get you in prison,or even killed. It's a very dangerous scam to carry out. Women who do this are not gold diggers at all. This is a very low-budget, shady hustle and it should not be attributed to the gold digging game at all. Like I said, a true-to-the-game gold digger uses her mouthpiece and her game to get everything she wants from a target. If she doesn't get it, she moves onto the next target. There's a target being born every minute in the United States alone. There's always opportunity in the game.

You don't have to scam, and you don't have to get over on anyone. You don't have to steal from anybody. You don't have to put yourself or your target in jeopardy in order to get money. If you do, you're in the wrong business. Again, a true to the game gold digger always uses her integrity and her game to get what she wants. A true gold digger is fair about the game. It's all about karma. Karma is very real. You don't want to be the kind of person who attracts negative karma by stealing from anybody or getting over anybody in a negative way. That kind of person will end up paying a price that is much greater than what she thought she gained in the first place. A true gold digger is going to keep her game straight and have good karma come to her. If she's in it for the long haul, she's going to do the right thing. Karma is reciprocal. If you do good things, good things will come to you. That is a fact. What comes around goes around. So put your best foot forward when you go for the gold.

*Gold Digger* CHECK LIST #9

**TOP 5 DESIGNER BAGS FOR GOLD DIGGERS**

1. LOUIS VUITTON SURYA XL BAG
2. ZAC POSEN ALEXIA HANDBAG
3. PRADA FRAME BAG
4. FENDI "B" BAG
5. MARC JACOBS CAROLYN CROCODILE HANDBAG

## "I STILL HAVE MY FEET ON THE GROUND, I JUST WEAR BETTER SHOES."

### — OPRAH WINFREY

# *Chapter Ten*

## TAILORING YOUR GAME ACCORDING TO RACE

Now that you have a general understanding about the gold digging game, I'm going to give you a couple of quick tips that you can use to enhance and spice your game up when you're out there in the field. One tip that I want to give is tailoring your game according to race. Even though the gold digging game is universal, the game can be used on any target from any ethnic background. Any female gold digger from any racial background can use the game as long as she abides by the principles and the rules of the game and play the game fair and accordingly. You can still tailor your game to certain niche targets. You can target certain ethnic groups and certain nationalities that will enhance your game. With certain ethnic groups, you will have a better chance of getting your foot in the door than with others.

Now, as far as race, men are usually intrigued by something that's exotic to them. Many rich men from different backgrounds want to experience things that people from their background normally don't experience. They want to experience different cultures. Rich men are very particular about trying out and tasting and dabbling in different cultures. Men from different nationalities always want to try out or deal with women from different nationalities. That makes the experience that much more exotic. That makes it more alluring. Generally,we are so used to seeing people from our own ethnic backgrounds, we often times take them for granted. But if you go to another country or another location, the people seem very exotic and vice versa. To better illustrate this, I've been down to Brazil and to me, the women are drop dead gorgeous. I am just in awe of the women down there. Ironically, the men from Brazil are very nonchalant about the women. They are used to seeing those women everyday, so it's no big deal to them. It's just a matter of perspective. It's the same thing when men from different backgrounds are dealing with women from your nationality or from your ethnic background.

The following is a list of how different women from different nationalities can work with targets from other nationalities and different racial backgrounds:

### #1: White Gold Diggers

Now, a lot of white females, especially the blondes, will have a lot of luck with men from the Middle East. You have a plethora of Middle Eastern oil guys and real estate tycoons coming to America all the time. Many rich Arab guys come over to America and their whole thing is to get a blonde white female on their arm. They want that white trophy wife. They're enthralled and intrigued with the iconic, western female blonde. If you're a white female, and looking for a special niche in the gold digging game, you would do very well with the rich Middle Eastern gentlemen with the oil money, or the sultan-type guys of Dubai.

Of course, white females would do well domestically, with regular American tycoons and other rich guys. But your game will really be enhanced, and you will seem that much more special and intriguing to a man who's from a different culture. Rich guys from the Middle East - I'm talking about billionaires - they sit up and watch television. They watch reruns of "Baywatch" and they see the white female icon of beauty, and they're very intrigued with that, and they want to experience that when they come over here. These guys are very, very good targets for white female gold diggers.

Also, white gold diggers would do well with Asian businessmen. Many Asian businessmen love American white females, especially blondes. They adore them. If you're a white female gold digger, you should target Asian businessmen because many of them watch western television  and they're very intrigued with western culture, particularly the dating scene. They too, like the idea of the white trophy wife.

White gold diggers should also consider black businessmen. They would do very well with older, black businessmen especially. They have a thing for white females, and good gold diggers will do real well targeting those gentlemen.

### #2: Asian Gold Diggers

Many rich American businessmen men have the submissive Asian girl fantasies burned into their subconscious minds. Asian girls would do very well with white businessmen in the United States. Many of these guys are very intrigued by the submissive, "catering to the man" vibe that the majority of Asian women are perceived to have. That's the stereotype that many people have about Asian women. Again, when it comes to dating different people of different nationalities, you're almost selling the stereotype to a certain degree. I'm talking about the positive stereotypes, not the negative ones. And the stereotype many people have about Asian girls is that they're very submissive and docile, willing to cater to the man's every whim, socially and sexually. That intrigues many rich guys. Aware of this already, Asian gold diggers are up on game. They come over to the states and date wealthy white guys. Moreover, there are many Asian and Pacific Island females who are mail-order brides to middle class white guys. But if you're an Asian gold digger, it's very good to target the wealthy white guys in America.

### # 3: Latina Gold Diggers

Latina gold diggers will have a great time catering to wealthy white and African American men in the states, because Latina women are prized for their perceived passionate sexuality. Many American men have that spicy, hot-blooded Latina fantasy thing going on. To them, there's nothing like a sexually explosive Latina girl. And again, we've had the pop culture phenomenon dubbed "the Latin explosion" here in America over the last decade. Many Latina singers and entertainers have been in the spotlight and in the media like J-Lo, Shakira, Eva Mendez, Rosalyn

Sanchez, and Salma Hayek, etc. Rich American men are intrigued by that spicy, sexy, Latina image. As a Latina gold digger, you would do very well with wealthy white and black businessmen and entertainers.

### # 4: Black Gold Diggers

Now, many black females in America complain that the ballers and rich guys-especially in the black community-like to date women of other races. Like I said before, many men like to date women who are exotic or foreign to them when they have money. They like to experience things that people from their background don't normally experience.

Often, when black men attain financial wealth, they like to experience things that they're not used to. Black women need to learn how to do the same in the gold digging game. They need to stop complaining about being left out. A lot of sistas complain about white women getting all the rich men, Latina women getting all the ballers, etc. Then they'll go so far to complain that all the *light-skinned* black women are getting the rich men. A lot of sistas have to really, really focus on expanding their horizons. As a black gold digger, you shouldn't just limit yourself to one section of the game. For a lot of black women in America, their main focus is to get at a rapper or a ball player.

The truth is, there are so many people with money besides those two types. That's why when you go to places like All-Star Weekend or Hip Hop events, you'll see a lot of black women congregating there. That's very limiting, because that's just short money. If you want to expand your horizons, you may have to go out of the country. I always tell sistas that many of them would do very well in Europe. If you are an in-shape, dark, American black woman, you will thrive in Europe. As a matter of fact, the darker you are, the better. In America, many dark skinned black women complain that they can't get access to the rich guys. They complain that they don't get the same kind of attention other women get. But over in Europe, it's a parallel universe.

Over in Europe-France, Italy, England, Spain, etc. - it's a chocolate gold diggers paradise because the men there love slim, in-shape, dark black women. A lot of sistas already know the game. Probably the first sista who understood that part of the game was Josephine Baker. She was a singer and entertainer who moved to Europe in the 1920s. She was a huge sensation there, especially in France. She became a French citizen in 1937. They loved her, because they weren't used to seeing a talented, exotic woman like that. They weren't accustomed to seeing an African-American woman who was so beautiful.

Many other women followed suit. Women like Diana Ross. Whenever we've seen her, she was always married to some European billionaire. Take Grace Jones. She rose to fame in the late 1970s and early 1980s as a model and singer. She was slim and dark-skinned, and married a few rich European guys. Another woman worth mentioning is Naomi Campbell. They absolutely love her in Europe. In countries like France and Italy, she's practically an icon over there. The singer Kelly Rowland from the group Destiny's Child is another woman who's very popular in the dating scene with rich guys. She's been associated with billionaire Richard Branson and other European rich guys.

In the south of France, St Tropez and the French Riviera are great spots for black women to go to and really, really come up in the game. Trust me, if you go over there, and you're a black woman from America, you will come up on a millionaire or a billionaire by accident. Again, in Europe, the game is wide open for black women, but a lot of them don't know this. The reason is simple: black women are constantly bombarded by images in the media what the standard of beauty is. But the standard of beauty worldwide varies. So I always tell sistas to go over to Europe, especially France, Italy, and England, and they will come up over there.

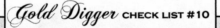 CHECK LIST #10

### TOP 5 JEWELRY ACCESSORIES FOR GOLD DIGGERS

1. CARTIER WATCH
2. BVLGARI NECKLACE
3. JAMES ALLEN DIAMOND RINGS
4. HARRY WINSTON EARRINGS
5. TIFFANY BRACELET

# THE *Art* OF GOLD DIGGING

## CONCLUSION

Finally, I want to talk about the art of mating. When you date, the person you date is either going to be an asset or a liability. The average couple gets into an asset/liabity based relationship. Just to give a quick overview of what an asset and a liability are in terms of relationships, imagine someone is having a party. An asset is a person who comes to the party and brings food,snacks,drinks,etc, and shares those treats with everybody. A liability is a person who comes to the party empty-handed. That person eats up all the food and drinks, and after everything is gone, he or she leaves. And that's really the state of modern relationships. This is why many relationships don't grow to their fullest potential, because one person has to take up the slack for the person who's the liability in the relationship. If somebody's not bringing something to the table, automatically he or she is going to take something from the table and you're going to have to pick up their slack. People can't grow like that. When a relationship like this runs it's course, you look back in hind site and you notice that nobody has accomplished anything. Everything either becomes stagnant or remains neutral. People lose out.

You have to understand that mating is not only an art but it's a science as well. Rich people understand it. This is why rich people date other rich people. This is why well off or moderately rich people date and marry up in class. This is why people like John Kerry married the woman from the Heinz fortune. This is why people like John McCain married the woman from the Anheuser-Busch empire. This is why rich actors date rich actresses. This is why Prince Charles, coming from the British royal family, married Diana, from another well-connected British family. This has been going on since the beginning of recorded civilization.

The Egyptians were the first ones to understand the concept of asset on asset dating. The Egyptian kings understood that if one of them came from a certain amount of wealth, he should marry a female who comes from another family of wealth. They put those assets together to grow and build so they could insure financial security for their bloodline. Rich people know how to nurture and breed family bloodlines like thoroughbred horses. A prime example is Arnold Schwarzenegger and Maria Shriver. These people came from wealthy backgrounds—he from the bodybuilding and entertainment world and she from the political world. Arnold, a Republican, and Maria, a Democrat, are from two different sides of the political world. But they intrinsically understood the bloodline of wealth.

To be a true to the game gold digger, you have to understand that bloodline of wealth as well. Like I said, the Egyptians were the first ones to really build on that bloodline of wealth. European kings and queens followed suit with this ideaology as well. Many of the kings coming from European royal families married women from royal families. Moreover, the kings of France, the kings of England—to name a couple—had mistresses. Yes, these kings had jumpoffs— women that they laid up with, otherwise known as courtesans. Of course, they never married their mistresses or jumpoffs in most cases. Those kings were very particular about who they procreated with to insure the wealth and the bloodline of the family. This is how they kept wealth within the bloodline. This is how they stayed rich for generation after generation after generation. They understood the concept of assets on assets. There was one family in particular, the Rothschilds, who was considered one of the richest families in the world. The men of that family were so serious about keeping the wealth within their bloodline, they would marry their cousins. This would truly insure their wealthy bloodline. This is how serious these people were about keeping that money and wealth in the family.

In many cases, poor people procreate with other poor people,therefore they never break the cycle of poverty that goes on for generation after generation.

If you're a female and are not from a wealthy family or prestigious background, you should still learn game from the people you date— especially from rich men. Try to become an asset. If you're trying to obtain or sustain a real relationship, try to bring something to the table. And when you date wealthy men, you should always date around first to really get your feet wet in the game. This will help you learn how to be around wealthy people. Don't try to be too serious with the first wealthy guy you date, especially if you have been out of the dating scene for a while. There are too many women sitting around waiting like Cinderella. They're waiting for a Prince Charming to come and rescue them, to come and take them away from their life of poverty/ abuse/boredom, etc. But the thing is, you have to get out there and work your game yourself. Your game is like a muscle. If you don't work the muscle, the muscle is going to atrophy and get weak. This is why when some people get out of the dating game, they say that their game is rusty. You have to get out there and work that game and learn how to work that muscle. Date a number of rich guys. This doesn't mean have sex or lay up with everybody. But just get into the dating scene with rich guys to be around that wealthy vibe, to learn from them, and to make contacts through them. You'll learn how to deal with rich guys and you'll learn how to be an asset when that one Prince Charming does come into your life and you want to have that long-lasting relationship.

There's a female by the name of Tracy Edmonds. She was in a video where she met the Grammy-winning, platinum-selling R&B

singer-songwriter Babyface. She ended up dating this guy. They got married and remained so for a number of years. And instead of just settling to be the pretty trophy wife, Tracy got around Babyface and learned the record business. She became a media mogul herself. Today, she's very respected in the entertainment community. She didn't just sit back and think that being a pretty girl is going to be her only asset. Sadly, that's a mistake too many women make. Tracy Edmonds learned quickly and soaked up the game. The she used the game for her benefit. Now she is a top notch female because not only is she beautiful, she has something to bring to the table.

Remember, ladies, when you date, do not think that your only job is to look pretty. If that's the only asset you're bringing to the table, at some point in time you're going to be replaced. If you're thinking about being with a wealthy person for the long haul, you have to soak up game, and be a real asset to the relationship. If you're going to be in a long-lasting relationship, try to contribute and build on that relationship. After all, being a pretty woman will get your foot in the door, but being a pretty woman with a lot of game to back up your looks will get you in the door and keep you in the game.

# ABOUT THE AUTHOR

**TARIQ "KING FLEX" NASHEED** is an author/lecturer and television personality who has appeared on TV shows such as The Tonight Show with Jay Leno, Late Night with Conan,and several shows for MTV and VH1. He is also the host of the critically acclaimed Mack Lessons Radio Show (macklessonsradio.com). Tariq does lectures all around the country teaching men and women his strategies and techniques on dating and relationships. Tariq lives in Los Angeles,Ca.

## CONTACT INFO FOR KING FLEX:
### KFLEX4LIFE@YAHOO.COM

**WWW.MACKLESSONS.COM**

**WWW.MACKLESSONSRADIO.COM**

**WWW.KINGFLEX.TV**

**WWW.MYSPACE.COM/TARIQ_NASHEED**

**WWW.THEARTOFMACKIN.COM**

**WWW.THEARTOFGOLDDIGGING.COM**

OTHER BOOKS BY
TARIQ "KING FLEX" NASHEED:

*THE MACK WITHIN
(PENGUIN)

* PLAY OR BE PLAYED
( SIMON AND SCHUSTER)

* THE ART OF MACKIN
(G.D. PUBLISHING)

## OTHER BOOKS BY
## TARIQ "KING FLEX" NASHEED:

# THE ART OF MACKIN'

229 pages

Publisher: G.D Publishing -King Flex Ent

**"(This book)comes from the experiences of a seasoned veteran of the game" -- Kronick Magazine, March 2001**

**"A much needed book" -- Dave Shaftel,The Source Magazine**

THE ART OF MACKIN' takes a fun, yet serious look at modern male/female relationships from an urban point of view. The ART OF MACKIN' is the first "how to book" that teaches men how to actually become "players" and "macks."

## OTHER BOOKS BY
## TARIQ "KING FLEX" NASHEED:

# THE MACK WITHIN

Paperback: 176 pages

Publisher: Riverhead Trade

The Art of Mackin' was the first book of rules for players-from overcoming fears of getting dissed to spotting a stank dead on. Now the expert on mackin' is back with the ultimate straight-up guide for every mack and mack-wannabe. Whether he's after ass or cash, trying to spit game at a Benz-driving Diamond Girl or a street-tough Copper Chick, or if he's just tired of being coochie-whipped, it's time to open up this book and unlock the time-tested secrets of the mack game.

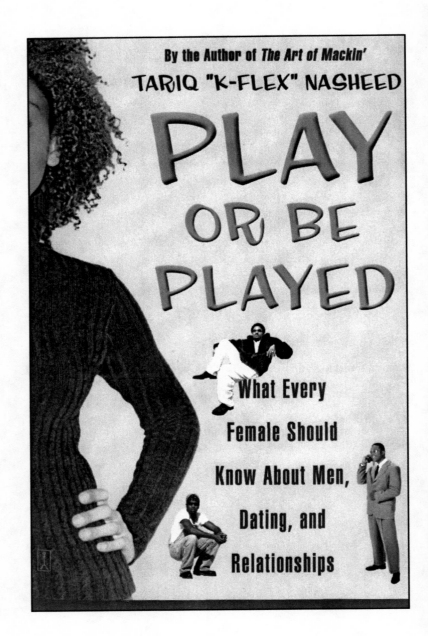

By the Author of *The Art of Mackin'*

## TARIQ "K-FLEX" NASHEED

# PLAY
# OR BE
# PLAYED

What Every
Female Should
Know About Men,
Dating, and
Relationships

## OTHER BOOKS BY
## TARIQ "KING FLEX" NASHEED:

# PLAY OR BE PLAYED

224 pages

Publisher: Fireside

## Got Game?

It's a fact. Every woman needs game. Take Oprah, Jada Pinkett-Smith, and Beyoncé Knowles. All three of these women have the one intangible quality that every mack, male or female, must possess: they all have game. In other words, they have intelligence, hustle, and common sense that they apply to every aspect of their lives -- especially in their relationships.

Play or Be Played is an instruction manual for women who are tired of being played by men and who want to be players themselves. Though women may not want to play games, the truth is men often do. So women who hope to win in the game of love must first learn the rules. Bestselling author and true mack, Tariq "K-Flex" Nasheed shares:

ways to spot a scrub
what it takes to get with a baller
why men cheat
how men really judge women
the top three mistakes women make in relationships
Street-smart and straightforward, Play or Be Played will help you get with a king without being a hoochie, groupie, or a chickenhead.

COMING SOON:

THE FIRST NOVEL FROM
TARIQ "KING FLEX" NASHEED

# THE GAME ADVISOR

Based on a true story.

## COMING

## SUMMER 2009!

# MACK
## LESSONS

LaVergne, TN USA
09 September 2009
157403LV00001B/157/P